The Accidental Wizard

By Simon Ludgate

18th February 2006

I'm sitting on my mum's bed, holding her hand. I notice it looks the same as mine but it's as if the plug has been pulled out. The air has escaped and it resembles a claw. Jean Niddrie Pitt, was Ludgate, nee Hubble. A lifetime in three surnames. It strikes me I'm very inappropriately dressed. I'm wearing a black, faded Adidas track suit with three stripes down the top and the pants.

I spilt some bleach on it a while ago and it's stained. It's not that I can't afford a new one, I just love this one. Like my Mum. I love her and she is also old. 75. She is dying. In an hour she will be dead and gone forever. I panic. I don't want her to go. I'm thinking about that depressing existentialist novel by Albert Camus, the Outsider. He couldn't remember if his mother had died that day or yesterday. He knew she was dead but couldn't remember. Shock or just forgetfulness?

My mind is wandering while my mum prepares to die. I don't want this to happen. I don't want her to leave me. I wish I'd dressed up. The direction of my life is going to change in 47 minutes for good. I can't see.

I am crying. I am crying a lot. I am sobbing my heart out like someone has died. What am I thinking? Someone is about to die. For real. She will sail across the sea to the angels, to the spirit guides, to her own Dad, Jack. I can feel him, I can smell his pipe. I can see his craggy old face breaking into a huge grin. He loves his daughter. And so he should.

She is the only woman I've ever known who hasn't gone weird after they turn 40 – well, apart from when she hit the menopause and I found her kissing Dave Olley one of my best friends at the time. Why do women turn so strange? I love women. I adore them. I have about 200 female friends and three males. But women seem to stop knowing what they want and whatever it is, it is always what you haven't got. And if you get it, they don't want it anymore. They wake up one morning and look at you and can't remember what you are for or what you are doing next to them. And when they tell you something, you know they are thinking something different .

That I do know as I have a gift. Or a curse. Jury's out. You see I know what people are thinking. I know if people are bad or good. I know if they have a guilty secret or sometimes if they going to die soon – something we are forbidden to ever say. That's a confession and a half on your Mother's deathbed isn't it? But it's her fault. She gave it to me as she is the same. She

2

rings you and asks you what's wrong. Or just turns up, expectant and knowing. Why? And how? I never wanted to be the same. But I do have it. Like lupus or bingo wings or short legs.

Which I have. Short legs that is. And I'm a bit chubby like her. My parents sat me down once when I was sixteen and told me I had a nice smile. I was going through my first really bad bout of depression, which is called being bi-polar these days. So at least I have that. My smile I mean, not depression although I secretly embrace my dips. I think of my smile as my angel. When I smile you can see my angel. When I get angry the devil rides out. I'm working on it.

I can feel the beautiful feathered wings on my back under the track suit. I could unfurl them and flap right away right now. I dream about it often enough. Maybe I'll get a tattoo? Right, shut it. Concentrate. I can't. That black cat sitting on the end of Mum's bed is purring too loudly. My mum says through closed eyes that the cat knows she is going. It curls up on the bed of patients in the hospice when they are about to die and it is never, ever wrong. Well that's settled. Mum asks me to leave as she needs to concentrate.

Fuck a doodle doo.

When have you ever heard an OAP ask for space to 'concentrate' when they are about to die? They usually say something like 'is that you dear?' or 'I can hear the sea'. Concentrate? Oh well. Suppose we had better go. But I know the moment I am out the door she will die and that will be it. I can't bear it. I start crying again.

I feel five. I feel five most of the time. Apart from when I get angry then I feel like Conan the Barbarian. I destroyed a whole free standing wardrobe once with my bare hands.

I'm scared of myself. It's a power inside me which is hiding. I feel I could push a building over by looking at it. I leave. The purring is louder. Bye bye dear she says. Not sure if she's talking to the cat or me. Probably the cat. She always loved animals.

My Mum and my daughter Tommy before Mum got really sick.

Mum, Jean Hubble, a month before she died.

18th March 2006

My Mum was a healer. People used to turn up on her doorstep unannounced so she opened a clinic where they could go.

I'm sitting at her funeral while her life flashes before me.

Why does that happen? Why does anything happen? I think I'll try to find out. Something strange is going on. Mum has only been dead a few days but I feel different somehow. I'm scared, tick. Confused, tick. Abandoned, tick.

But a door is starting to open. This is very, very strange. It's as if she has closed one door behind her but opened one in my mind. She's been doing that all my life. Without me really noticing. There was this spiritual powerhouse hiding in a little old lady. Don't get the wrong idea. She wasn't a weed. She'd step up to the plate when she had to. Before she got cancer she had arms like tugboats which is where I got mine from. And she had a temper on her when she was younger.

Did you know the Nephilim (Biblical giants like Goliath) were supposed to be retrieved miscarriages? My mum had five. She chased me up the stairs with a poker hot and glowing from the fire once. Her eyes were burning like coals too. That stopped when I grew up a bit and she had to look upwards to tell me off as I'd start laughing. She looked so funny. Anger in a short, fat woman is pure comedy. But she loved me, treasured me, as she saw her gift mirrored and wanted to teach me her ways. The ways of a psychic, a visionary, an enlightened teacher. OK. I got that. But I didn't want it. But maybe I do now? Maybe I'm ready? Maybe I will walk out of her funeral and kill myself, maybe not.

Abandonment. That's the one which defeats me. Whenever I'm abandoned, I can feel my strength ebbing away like Superman suffering the effects of Kryptonite.

It's odd how you can go from super happiness to abject misery as fast as you can blink your eyes. I do it all the time. An unguarded comment, or worse, a thought. Or a certain look in someone's eyes and you just know. You've taken the bait before they even realize you've understood what they have just said. Everyone feels the need to over-explain everything.

It's OK. I get it. Usually before you've finished the sentence. It's the handshake when I meet a stranger. I just know. It would make my life, and others, easier if I kept that to myself. But it's time you knew. Now my Mum is dead and I can't hide behind her, I need to come clean. This is a very strange state of mind. Why does it take her dying for me to start living? I'm so bad at it.

The radio receiver in my head twirls through channels constantly. It picks up other people's pain. The impact and shock of a train crash on another continent, the sickening pain of a cruel bayonet or knife in the guts, anger, joy, pain. It strikes me from nowhere. My mood never matches the circumstances and then sometimes I watch the news and understand where it came from. My life is like wearing a suit and trainers at a greyhound track with someone else's gorgeous wife in tow. Mismatched and chancing it but nothing can fight off the constant abstract sad feeling inside.

I want to be happy and content but I never have been and maybe never will. Low seratonin levels apparently. I want to fit in but I never have. I love my wife. I really do. My mind has wandered again. My daughter Tommy is singing 'Somewhere Over The Rainbow'. She is beautiful and so is that song. Never be able to listen to it again though. I feel my Mum sitting on the rafter above.

She is young and luxuriant again with thick red hair. She is swinging her legs like a kid. She is a kid. She is going to be off soon but just wanted to make sure everyone was OK - just like she always did. Well I'm not Mum. I feel like a ship which has slipped its mooring in a storm, torn the ring from the jetty on the end of the painter line and is now dragging it in the water. I start crying again. I have to learn to deal with death, I really do. That's my mission. Apart from discovering who or what I am.

Maybe it's time I faced that too. I'm standing looking down into Mum's open grave. She's in a little wicker basket like a baby. Moses. I like the idea of being Moses. I think I'll re-read the Old Testament. Have you ever done that like reading a novel? My God. What a violent, vengeful God the Old Testament God was. That can't be right, surely? They seemed to spend their time lopping heads off their enemies, their wives, girlfriends, even children and chucking them over the city walls.

I wouldn't be surprised if the family dog, hamster and goldfish went too. What is that about? Why would the creator of the Universe want someone's goldfish bunged over a wall? Do you think God created goldfish for revenge? No. Course not. Does that make the Old Testament bunk? Possibly.

The Book of Revelations is pretty trippy though. It's the last convulsion of the New Testament and is proving to be the soundtrack for the 21st century, as far as I'm concerned. My suggestion is that's the one to have a flick through – you might recognise the occasional world leader, an anti-Christ or two or a natural hazard. It predicts a set of holy figures will emerge from the Pit posing as Jesus, Moses and angels, who will then kill everyone.

I make documentaries about disasters. Great for your state of mind, I can tell you. Maybe that's why I'm so depressed? It may be, but right now it's because I'm standing tossing a handful of earth on my Mother. I want to get down in the hole and curl up with her like I used to when I was a child. Dad knew his job was to swap and sleep in my bed. Wished that still worked with other women.

What am I saying? Am I Oedipal as well? Oh God. I can't move. My feet are growing into the soil like a tree. I wonder how long it will be before she decomposes into soil herself? Will her skull burst through the ground while she dances to Thriller? She can dance now. She's free. That must be a happy thought. Come on Simon, pull yourself together!

Nope.

Still feel as miserable as shit.

Mum's last resting place. I like the Angels bit. My sister Tracy came up with that.

23rd March 2006

Things I like: Science. Broken lawnmowers. The feel of my wife's lips when she kisses me. Grapes. The mysteries of the Universe. Quantum Physics. Astronauts. Barry Sheen. Speed. Looking in someone's mind. It's official then. I am a five year old deviant with an IQ.

Have you ever been to a meeting of MENSA members? Probably not if you have any sense. Pick up club for old men who like chasing young brainy girls. So they aren't that stupid then but they do seem to be incapable of understanding even the simplest psychic truth. I am even more sad than I was at the funeral, which is not encouraging. I am developing long-term depression and am more bi-polar than ever. I have written a list of things I want to put right.

My Mum told me an angel lives above Glastonbury Tor and it's a portal, whatever that is. She also said I should visit the College of Psychic Studies. She's been gently programming me for years and years to prepare me. How beautiful is that fact? I love that. Makes me feel like a wizard. Actually I suspect I might be a wizard. Or an angel. Or a demon.

How is it possible to get those mixed up? Well, I have. Which is worrying. When I was baby, or very young, angels and demons used to come into my room. Sometimes I felt the love and light of the angels and other times there was darkness and cold fear. The angels had soft, shining faces and they floated in the air. The demons clumped like horses with hooves and were very ugly and angry.

My ears would whistle, though not both sides at once, rather one at a time. Then I would spin round in my cot til I was a blur and would leave with whoever had come for me. I think I might have some sort of natural weapon in me. They might have put it there. Like the staff of Aaron, or the ark of the covenant. Something unseen, run on divine energy. I have no idea why or why it should be there. My brother would tell me I was imagining it. Maybe I am. Maybe I will use it on him first. Only kidding Pete, love you really. At least you give a shit.

Glastonbury Tor, Somerset, England. My special place. My magic place.

14th May 2006

I am an ordinary, unremarkable person. I don't pretend to have any specialist spiritual knowledge. But I do pick up a lot of information along the way. I am intuitive. Sensitive. I seem to know things I can't remember being told or learning. Past life memory? Possibly. Connected to the higher collective conscious? Steady matron. I travel a great deal. I have a very enquiring mind. I have a natural ability to understand how things work. When science runs out of answers, I like to start making up my own.

Scientists see this as a very bad thing indeed. Richard Dawkins detests it if anyone should dare to which is why he distrusts religion and I don't blame him for it. But he is missing out on the joy of enlightenment. Sure, he can bask in intellectual and factual certainty and that is his truth but I suspect there is more. And I want to know what that is. I want to embrace it. To own it.

 I am talking about the spiritual. I want to feel sure in my own mind whether or not there is a God, whether we are alone and forsaken or not. Why there are so many references to angels in our cultures? Everyone from Robbie Williams to the Prophet talk about them. (Alright Rob?) So there must be something in it as I respect both sources big time. I've started reading books on the subject. New Age spiritualism type stuff. It talks about the sort of thing my Mum was always going on about. I am not a hippy.

I am also not a tree hugger. Although I did try it and it felt good. But don't tell anyone that. My sister Tracy just told me she has had conversations with fully formed people who are dead. She had a conversation with her dead father-in-law whom she has never met. He had his face an inch from hers when she woke up in the middle of the night which was startling, to say the least, and when she went down to the kitchen the cups on the Welsh Dresser were swinging, which they do for no reason quite regularly. When she turned round he was sitting at the table. He told her things which she woke her startled husband up and told him. Weird.

Archangel Metatron on the roof of my house.

Some Thoughts From Now Before We Progress Any Further With The Story

A word about angels. They are going to figure in this little chat you and I are having so I wanted to tell you what I know about some of them now. I'm cheating a bit in my own chronology but this might help. Uriel, Metatron and Michael are my closest angelic guides which is a powerful team. Uriel appears in my photographs as a white hexagonal shape. Often in the exact centre of the photo. Michael sometimes merges with him, giving the image a blue tinge. Metatron is huge and milky with a red and orange edging to his shape. Angels are omnipresent and can appear to as many people as they like at the same time. They can, and will, do anything. Uriel is the angel of floods and earthquakes which is appropriate really as I have spent so much time documenting both. Metatron is connected very, very powerfully to God itself.

He is also the angel of death in that he is responsible for the Stellar Gateway, the bridge to Heaven, and he holds the Akashic record. This is the record of everything. Every breath, act, deed, blade of grass, atom. Everything. It's why people say their life flashed before them when they have a near death experience.

They step into the Akashic record between life and death and start to see their contribution. Souls who are reluctant to face it often get stuck and wander the earth as spirits such is their desire not to face the music as it were. Metatron was incarnated as Enoch, or Elijah in the Talmud, and is the only angel to have walked the earth as a man apart from his twin brother Sandalphon which literally means twin brother in Greek. Only angel to have walked the earth, apart from the Nephilim, who are fallen angels and a bit naughty. We'll get to them later.

Metatron and Sandalphon understand what it means to experience pain, fear and hunger physically. Michael is the comforter to people who have lost their way or conviction or who suffer from some sort of addiction. His sword is used for cutting the snares of entrapment and is the ally of exorcists.

Raphael is the angel of healing and cure and Chamuel is the angel of love. There are many angels and everyone finds they work with different ones. You just know when they are around, who you are close to and what they represent. But there are also plenty of books, and our friend Google, where you can find out everything you need to know. You will find it is very consistent.

Uriel. This was the first time I saw him on my roof.

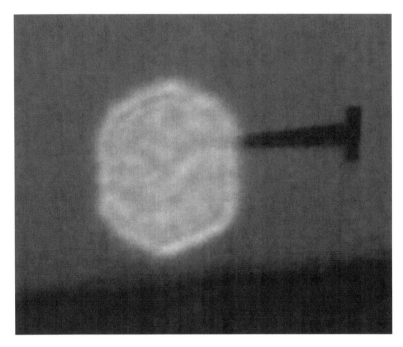

And this is the same shot blown up.

I am beginning to realize I have visited a surprisingly high proportion of the areas around the planet which are deemed portals and earth chakras. And I'm just a bloke from Chiswick, London who makes science programmes for telly.

I'm on a personal spiritual mission and I want to know things but I suspect you are more interested in hearing what happens next rather than me trying to explain it all.

In a world first for modern media I am going to assume you are extremely intelligent and well-informed. I am not going to treat you like a baby or an idiot 'cos that's how everybody else is made to treat their audience. The media think you are too stupid to think for yourself but that won't be applicable here.

If you do start feeling a bit bamboozled or lost can I suggest you refer to the internet? I didn't set out to be a substitute for Wikipedia in writing this book! Great thing the internet – the externalization of our nervous system as Marshall McLuhan called it. The theory goes the earth is just like us and has concentrations of energy like we do in our own bodies but in relation to the planet, energy is released from an area called middle earth. But you will have to think for yourself.

Scientists refer to the belt where spacecraft orbit as middle earth. Maybe they are right. Maybe our electro magnetic outer blanket around the earth is where the earth's energy is stored? Makes sense as it is measurable and the earth is not hollow. It also makes sense with your own body energy. And my scientific mind is thinking about the importance of the electro magnetic shields around the earth.

Electro magnetism is very important and I recommend you try to learn as much about it as possible. When I was making a show about the Bermuda Triangle we reflew the legendary Flight 19 route to see what effect electro magnetism might have had on their disappearance. Flight 19 famously disappeared just after World War 2 ended while they were flying a routine mission out of Fort Lauderdale in Florida. We found an Avenger, identical to the planes which disappeared, and flew the same route.

At the same time as the original squadron reported having problems with their instruments, which was 4.10 pm, we ran into problems. Same take off time, same course, same plane. It was very eerie indeed. Our turn and slip indicator froze, as did the compass. In both the Avenger and the modern plane filming us. I filmed this happening and we put it in the show. It felt very surreal.

We flew on for a few minutes with no compass but we were soon unsure about where we were. Which was exactly what happened to the original flight. Flight 19 flew on and became increasingly confused about where they were. They eventually ran out of fuel and ditched and were lost. We switched on the GPS compass and flew home but I experienced for myself what it feels like to be over water in a plane and not know which way is right.

With Fort Lauderdale in sight, I noticed five shiny objects wheeling above us. They were travelling very fast and it was virtually impossible to say what they were but they weren't anything I could categorise. I think these may have been my first UFOs.

We discovered that the Bermuda Triangle area has a 6% lower electro magnetic field than the rest of the planet thanks to the Danish Meteorological Office who were surveying the planet with a satellite at the time. They couldn't believe it either as that is a massive differential. 0.1% would be huge. 6% is almost unimaginable but there it was. No wonder compasses spin, people get lost and strange fogs appear in the Triangle!

The Avenger Bomber we flew round the Bermuda Triangle in. Its folded wings remind me of an angel.

Just to prove I was there, here I am in the navigator's seat in the Avenger somewhere over the Bermuda Triangle. I look confident but I had no idea where I was at that moment or if we would make it home. I pinched the hat off the station commander's desk at the Miami Coastguard station in Fort Lauderdale. Sorry Chief.

The chase plane filming me in the Avenger. Their instruments froze up at the same time ours did and we had to resort to modern GPS eventually as we had no idea where we were. Very uncomfortable feeling.

The Bermuda Triangle is notorious for mysterious crashes and disappearances. This wreck of a DC3 was on the sea bed off Nassau. This was an opportunity I couldn't pass up so we featured it in the show.

Back to chakras. You have seven chakras from the crown of your head to your bum hole to be specific. If you sit and think about how your head feels, your throat, your heart, stomach, or base, you will get this. These are

15

powerful things. And you have five more chakras on top of the seven which float above your head and below your feet. I have discovered I can feel when someone else has a problem with one of these areas of their chakras as they are so important in balancing the body. If someone has been ill, hanged, raped or stabbed or something in a previous, or indeed present, life I can generally tell..

1st September 2006 (we're back to the story now, ok?)

When I met my wife in 1991, she was my client. I started falling in love with her immediately. She is five feet four, unbelievably cute, with huge brown eyes which bore into you like lasers. Her short bobbed hair is brown and sleek. She has the prettiest feet I have ever seen. You can tell an awful lot about someone by the state of their feet.

She is a charming host and is a fascinating polyglot of Italian and Dutch heritage. She can speak four languages. She didn't speak a word of English til she was 16. Any trace of a foreign accent has been eradicated which is an indicator of her incredible ear for language and her intelligence. She has a very aristocratic Roman nose like Caesar had on ancient coins.

I wanted to marry her almost right away. The first time I shook her hand I felt she was Jewish, and a tragic Jew at that. I could feel her dying, struggling for breath and then being riddled with bullets. Nice. I still fell in love but the impression was disturbing.

She eventually admitted to having a recurring nightmare where she escapes from a room filling with water through a small window with her brother behind her. She swims out into water and she can see the sun above but is horrified to realise she is under a thick layer of ice and she drowns along with her brother, helpless.

In concentration camps the Nazis used Zyklon-B gas on prisoners.

They would be stripped naked and herded into a room with a small grate in the roof – the only source of light or air. Then Zyklon-B pellets would be dropped into the room through the grate. On exposure to the air, the pellets would become a deadly gas which was a development of the mustard gas used in World War 1. It would make the victim feel as if they were drowning as it paralysed the respiratory system as well as scarring it beyond use if anyone survived breathing it in. The poor souls who were killed like this would be found in a human pyramid as they died clawing their way to the light and the only source of oxygen. No such thing as evil? That's where I think my darling, beautiful wife met her fate in a previous life.

16

Before we get into the murky depths of my spiritual journey together, and it's my profound wish that it becomes a journey for you too where you end changed from how you began, there is something I want to say.

I am not a self-regarding person with an insufferable male ego - despite how it might look so far. I have issues with self-confidence and self-belief.

I over-compensate. I have always had a tendency to put the interests and happiness of others first. I am shy. So shy I couldn't pay for a cinema ticket or ice cream and I stuttered as a child. Bb-b-b-b-b-adly. But the process of writing something about your personal journey requires a fair amount of the first person singular. This is about me trying to find myself and not dissolve the way I have so many times in my life. And maybe this journey together will help you on a voyage of discovery too. I hope so.

Writing your first book – even if it's a diary like this - is also a bit like having your first new car. Metaphorically, you drive too fast and show off. I promise to try to calm down as we get further into this story and I settle in a bit.

I'm going to talk about some intensely personal stuff. So please be gentle with me as what I would like to explain to you might give you comfort about the meaning of your own life and its significance.

There's a rather bad bit at the end, just to warn you, but I can't do anything about the message – they've asked me to tell you and it is what it is. It's also supported in science and recent events. Sorry. But it's possibly the reason behind why they have woken me up and they would like to do something similar with you. It's a bit like pyramid selling for the soul. It's their fervent wish that you know about this too so we can collectively do something to stop or alter what is coming, and what is already here.

The earth is thought of as a divine feminine energy, Lady Gaia.

Not Lady Gaga, Gaia! She is growing in strength again at the moment and the ebb and flow of warming, cooling, flood, drought or earthquake is part of the natural cycle. It is also connected to solid scientific reasons but I see science and the spiritual as intertwined, not as separate camps.

With enough enlightened, positive thought and pure love in the heart, potential paths can be altered. Nothing is set in stone. Pre-determination doesn't make sense to me. Everything is a possibility until it happens, then it is done and we move on.

Lady Gaia has shrugged off land dwellers enough times in the past. Fossils, sedimentation, ice deposits, and the visible patterns of the rock in mountain ranges tell the story of past ice ages, of floods, blitzes from heat, global

17

warming and the end of species. 3.5 billion years of it. We have about another billion years before the sun swells into a red giant and consumes us but there is always the possibility of massive change in the interim.

I have seen enough of the damage natural disasters bring to comprehend what a tenuous grip we have on survival. Walking amongst the rubble of what was a town, a community, and was reduced to dust in a less than a minute, really brings that comprehension into focus. I think these experiences I have had in Indonesia, Pakistan, Haiti, Chile and Japan have shown me what nature can do.

There have been many experiences and lessons for me which have come out of this but what it has done is bring me closer to the angelic realm. There is always intense spirit activity in earthquake zones as they are active with recently deceased souls, angels of protection and Archangels who watch over the earth when it is turmoil.

There is a sense of something which is always the same in disaster areas. The sense of sorrow is mixed with an angelic calm. Archangel Metatron, Uriel, Michael, Rafael, Chamuel and Gabriel bring the strength and the tools to survive such calamity and I feel them with me whenever I walk amongst the rubble of what had been a town where hundreds, sometimes, thousands of unfortunate bodies lie crushed beneath tons of concrete.

After the Himalyan earthquake. Balakot, Pakistan, November 2005.

In Bagh, Pakistan at the other end of the fault line to Balakot in the Hindu Kush. November 2005.(Picture courtesy Geoff Price)

We hitched a ride in a US Army Reserve Chinook helicopter which just happened to be flying along the length of the fault line after the Pakistan earthquake. I was able to film a world exclusive showing the entire track of the earthquake from the air. I was so excited I very nearly fell out of that open window I was filming from when we made an unexpected tight turn. (Picture courtesy Geoff Price)

The angels can touch you at any time and as well as the more extreme moments in my life when I've been amongst the carnage of a recent tsunami or quake, something as simple as walking the dogs in Richmond Park in London can produce a meeting with one of them which is always a humbling experience. I think the way they appear is to match a form we can understand. In other words our own physical appearance of a human but with a celestial aura. Wings were added to explain their ability to levitate so as not to scare us and the interpretation stayed. They are believed to be radioactive which might explain biblical references to being burned by coming too close to them.

Kitty and I in our favourite place – Richmond Park, London. If you sit and look into my eyes in this picture for long enough you will connect to the Angels and maybe even start to take pictures of them yourself. I projected that wish as this was taken - especially for you! Kitty didn't mind what happened as long as I gave her a cheeseburger. She is the reincarnated soul of my third daughter who didn't make it. (Picture courtesy Maureen Barrymore)

13th September 2006

I'm about to tell you the moment when my spiritual quest starts, spurred by Mum dying. The actual, definable second it happens which is going to change my life and unfortunately lead to a series of mini-Crucifixions for me, which will not be very nice. But before I do, I want to talk about time.

We think in terms of everything being in a line. We're born, we live, we get kicked around, we get old, we get kicked around a lot more, we die, we become ash or turnips. The solar system rotates on its interlocuting axis as it moves through space. Time ticks away, never to be retrieved.

But what do you make of the fact that light, that most familiar entity, exists as *both a wave and a particle at the same time*? Huh? Yeah, that's right. It exists on two planes. And that can be demonstrated in a simple scientific experiment which I've just done for a programme on quantum physics. Yes, while light is washing ashore in a gently lapping wave at 186,000 miles per hour – ok so not so gentle then – it is bouncing around as photons which are like very, very tiny beads.

What's this got to do with the price of fish? Everything. Scientists will tell you how that one astounding fact makes the existence of multi dimensions possible. It suggests time could travel backwards or stop or that whole levels of existence could be hidden in different dimensions, accessible through worm holes or, in other words, tears between different times.

I am absorbing this myself after filming the experiment and meeting Uri Geller to interview him for my programme on the Bermuda Triangle. He seems to know this, and already understands and applies it. I ask him on the phone why I think of herds of black and white cows as we're driving to his mansion in Buckinghamshire.

It turns out the lawn is decorated with concrete black and white cows when we get there. That would be why then. He has a very, very powerful psychic electro-magnetic aura. Crikey, this man is not from planet earth. He really can bend metal. I see him do it with my own eyes from three inches away and there are no tricks.

He holds me in a psychic armlock for weeks after we meet. I can see him watching me. Oh, I forgot to mention that. I can see places where I'm not too. Sort of like being in two places at once – shit, like light itself. Of course! We must be our own particle wave accelerators!

I confess I am having fun writing this, freely, from my subconscious, guided by the angels, where anything and everything is going to surface. Can you please allow yourself to let go too and let's see what happens!? (Stephen Fry - this is addressed to you in particular for some reason) – anyway, this is proving to be a very cathartic experience for me – never mind you! - as when I write a voiceover script for a tv programme, every tiny detail must be explained and substantiated. Here I am going to say exactly what I like – but I have lots of photos to illustrate and maybe substantiate what I say, think and believe.

It once got so crazy substantiating or annotating our script for a tv science show, the network asked us to prove humans were actually bipeds so we sent them a picture of Missy's husband Morgan naked. I'll get to Missy later, but take it from me she is an angel on earth. We call her the General. And what I'm doing here with this diary is to take you through my personal spiritual journey as it happens with a ton of confusing, crazy notions and experiences.

What's amazing will be that you will get it because you are human and if you allow yourself to let science and spirituality coalesce and become one, like the seven rays of the spectrum become one white light when they mix, you will get it. And there will be pictures. Of things which make no sense but will stir memories in you about your deeply buried self.

A self, an "I am", a Monad, which is a light being, capable of time travel, travel on the astral plane, seeing remotely, hearing, feeling and sensing things which have always been there but you have forgotten how to sense. And we are 100% not alone. We are being watched, guided, loved and influenced by forces outside what we think we know. Got your attention? Good. Here's what happened to me then.

If you bought this book, and have got to this bit, you want to know more, right? Maybe you are looking forward to picking off what I say like clay pigeons instead which you can shoot down with a satisfying puff of clay dust. Or you are ready for some information you weren't expecting, knew might be there, or are actively needing to have it explained. Something is changing. The world is changing.

The world is in trouble. The food and the water is going to run out. Scientists are predicting we will need two planets' worth of food production by 2050 to feed the world's population. If we don't get a grip on contraception and give the world a rest from us, we will not survive. It is just not feasible. If we empower and educate women about contraception it could work. If we leave it to men, it won't. When I was born in 1957, the world's population was a little over 1.5 billion.

There are almost that many people in China now and the total global population is 7 billion. The Himalayan glaciers are melting so fast they could disappear within 20 years from now. Recently the UN and the International Panel on Climate Change have revised their prediction to be less Draconian but the point remains the same, water will become the subject of crisis and cause wars in the future.

The Himalayas provide 20% all of the world's fresh water. The Ganges in India, the Yellow River and Yangste River in China and the Mekong delta in Vietnam flood during the summer due to melwatwater from glaciers. The Human race is driving climate change and warming. Farting cows and melting tundra releasing CO_2 and methane is a diversion.

North America, India, Europe and China now produce 26 gigatonnes of CO_2 a year. That is too much. End of. Never mind what the oil industry and governments pay skeptics to say. It's too much and the earth can't absorb it. Sure, it's only 3% of the total CO_2 produced on the earth but it's a deal breaker. Nature deals in small percentiles. Parts per million of CO_2 have increased from 185 to 395 since the start of the industrial revolution. That sort of increase left to nature has taken 50 million years before, not just 200 years.

Scientists will tell you about ice core samples from the Arctic from thousands of years ago where similar levels of CO_2 have been found. It unbalances the climate and causes ice ages or confusingly catastrophic warming as with the Pleistocene ice age 11,000 years ago or the Cretaceous era burn out 50 million years ago. No ice in the latter obviously but they use rock and sediments to tell that story instead.

The Colorado River in the US which used to flow to the Pacific on the west coast doesn't make it anymore. Cities like Las Vegas suck the water out of the river until it dries up into a puddle. What has any of this to do with my spiritual journey or what sparked that moment in me?

Everything. I've been to glaciers in Alaska, Chile and the Arctic and they are shrinking or unwinding into the sea like a melting ice cream. I started taking these trips in association with my work long before I had my moment of awakening. It worries me deeply. I feel as if we are sleep-walking into really bad trouble without being conscious.

I want to know what I can do about it. What I can do to change our thinking. I want to know if there is anything out there apart from us who is involved, who can guide us, if there is a higher intelligence which might be able to change our collective consciousness for the better? Or are we doomed to spin through space until we starve or choke unguided and unaided?

For me, the spiritual change personally begins with an innocent looking photo of my best friend Mark mucking around with his daughter in their back garden. And change is what is needed. Everything is about change these days. Have you noticed?

15th February 2007

I am sitting looking at my photos on my computer. For some reason I have been thinking about angels again. I went out with my luminous friend Liz Bonnin last night. She and I had one of the most fun experiences of my life making a series called Gadgets and Stuff where Stuff Magazine fed us cool gadgets to feature and I could pick anything I fancied from the gadgets trolley. Every boy's dream.

Liz is a brilliant presenter and I'm secretly in love with her in a harmless adolescent way like every single one of her other male friends and we have a conversation about angels over dinner at Roko, my favourite restaurant on the planet. I tell her I think I'm an angel, literally. She takes it quite well but I can feel she thinks I may be a little mad. But I do. I really do. It may be a strong sense of Spirit or God or something in me but it is profound.

Back to the photo of my friend. For some reason I suddenly notice the little girl Robin has a sort of bubble right on her forehead. I look closer. I increase the magnification on the picture. And this is the moment. The defining moment. In a picture I've browsed through a dozen times, there is something there I've never noticed before. I run through every scenario I can based on working with pictures and film for 20 years. Lens flare? No light source apart from the flash as we were in a pitch black garden. Condensation? Possibly. Dust? Possibly.

It goes on. But there is a knowing in my consciousness, in my heart, my chakras, that it is none of these. The bubble has beautiful vanes and patterns like nothing I have ever seen before.

Mark and Robyn Mellor and the little orb which ignited my fascination with the subject and will totally change my life.

The same picture enlarged which shows that beautiful orb on Robyn's head more clearly.

30th April 2007

I ask a friend what the bubble might be. She says it is an orb. That is a word I have never heard used in that way before. I Google it and hundreds of references come up, including youtube videos and books on the subject. There are some nice looking ones written by someone called Diana Cooper. I order a few of her books on Amazon.

A piece in the puzzle has suddenly fallen into place. Before starting to look and research – something I love to do – I already know what the bubble is. It's intelligent, it's what we have referred to for millennia as an angel, it's saying hello to me as it is time I woke up and stopped messing around.

This thought pops into my head like a letter landing on the mat. Not there one moment, there the next - like it has always nestled comfortably in that spot. Strangely I have no recollection of who the friend is who tells me what they are. That happens a lot too – I am always meeting kind people who help me out of a jam or just tell me something I need to know at the time then I can't quite remember what they looked like later or even if they were male or female. I will come to recognise them as angels.

But don't think they are the only physical manifestation of what we are surrounded by. Other less positive forces are incarnated or can manifest from time to time. Once I learn to recognise them, I sometimes approach them and the evil in them comes off in waves. And they hate to be spotted. I walked right up to one of these characters and asked him where he was from. He looked startled and he replied "Persia". Not Iran please note. But the old country before the Imans made it Iran and started flogging women on the bare souls of their feet til they bleed just for being women or so it seems.

Angels of protection over Yosemite, California. One of my first from 2004.

6th June 2007

I'm searching through my pictures to check for any more of these orbs to see if this was a singularity or if there are others. There are more. My heart starts to thump (another sign I come to recognise as being in the presence of angels) as I look at a picture I took on a research trip to Yosemite, California. There are what look like two massive transparent pancakes floating in the air. And I instinctively know they are angels of protection. Protecting what? I ask to no one in particular. My ear is ringing. Spirits of North American Indians protecting the ancient burial ground at the base of the towering mountain comes the reply.

I just know that is the answer. Sorry Richard Dawkins, but I do. Richard Dawkins is sort of my scientific conscience. Evidence. Proof. Empirical observation. The doubts and mockery spin around in my head. I know it sounds daft and implausible but it is my truth. He'd probably say double light refraction. Decomposition in the salts in the CCD device in the camera which mimics the chemical reaction of traditional chemical film. Sweat? Dust? This is going to happen a lot and there is nothing I can do about it until something unequivocal comes along. But why isn't the same imperfection there on my photos in the same setting? Why isn't it there on the shot before or after?

When the lens cracks, or the O-Ring seals pop and let in moisture, the lens develops a permanent line or bloom on the bowl of one of the glasses. I know as I've had it happen when we flew from one location to another in Alaska in an unpressurised aircraft at 10,000 feet which then landed at 500 feet above sea level. The drop in pressure was enough to pop the seals and we had a halo in the centre of the $10,000 lens.

This is not that. I find a stupid picture of me dressed as Fred Flintstone from June 2004. There is a beautiful little blue orb by my hand. I already know it is Archangel Michael. My Mum always used to talk about Michael's blue protective cloak of light and his sword. I have no idea how she knew this and I never thought to ask. Bit late now. How can a whole Angel be present as a possible trick of the light next to my hand without me even knowing?

But I have always felt I was an angel myself and I was surrounded by others haven't I? So this is a revelation. I am scared and excited at the same time. Is this why I saw them as a baby? Why I dream about them? Why they seem to be in my pictures now? I feel like that kid in Close Encounters when ET lights up his finger! And I can tell you Mr Steven Spielberg was way ahead of me, as was Stanley Kubrick. Both of these amazing directors have already reached out and put their hand through the thin membrane which divides the dimensions and seen what lies behind. I am so blown away I can hardly breathe or sleep.

What to do? My wife takes the news like I've only just heard JFK was assassinated in Dallas 50 years ago or something. How can she be so calm? For the first time ever I start to see her as the angelic guide she is. How can I have not noticed before? How could I not have noticed? I love her so much. I look for other evidence and there it is. A beautiful picture of my younger daughter Betty and one of our pups, Luca. A white orb floats in the foreground.

 A diving shot of little orbs everywhere – yes, yes jellyfish I know. Course they are. Believe what you like. Whatever is your reality, man! Three Indonesian gentleman, who helped me out of a tight spot when we were filming after the Indonesian tsunami and who loaned me $5000, have a double orb on the pocket of the trousers with the money in. That's what I call an angel of protection. An angel of Brinks Mat?

27

An orb of protection on my friend Andrea's pregnant belly. It is looking after an unborn Jack. I'll come back to Jack a few times as we go – almost every picture of this little boy features a big orb. And then there is the Pakistan earthquake – faint orbs in the rubble. I told you I do disaster! How could I have missed them? Well we do. It's called paradigm blindness.

Orbs in the rubble of the Pakistan earthquake in November 2005 in Mushaffrabad. There are a faint line of them to the right.

I'm feeling expansive after a glass or two of wine so I'll help you out here. When Captain Cook landed in what became the Cook Islands, the locals couldn't recognise his ship as they had never seen one and their brains couldn't process the information – happens apparently with UFO sightings where one person sees it and the person next to them doesn't. The local shaman could see Cook's ship but no one else could. It wasn't until the crew walked right up to the islanders that they suddenly focused on them and they were sore afraid!

When Jack was in the womb there was an angel of protection close to him already. Look at the faint white orb floating where the unborn Jack is. Meet Gary and Andrea Gordon, my friends. Taken on Burns Night, November 2005.

My daughter Betty, Luca, and a passing orb in one of the photos I discovered from my own collection after I "woke up". This was taken in December 2005.

On a diving trip in May 2004 with an array of orbs across the bottom of the shot.

Jakarta, Indonesia, May 2005. There is a double orb protecting the pocket with the money in it. There is also a tiny one whizzing along at the top of the picture in the middle.

Fred Flintsone in January, 2004 with Archangel Michael by my left hand.

6th September 2007

I'm thinking about a drive I had to make across Arizona from Flagstaff to Window Rock in the far bottom corner of the state before it becomes New Mexico. I go via the Grand Canyon, therefore across the land of the Navajo Indians who own most of Arizona, and into the Hopi reservation and on to Monument Valley in Utah and back down to Window Rock, the HQ of the Navajo Nation. I'm scouting locations for our series on how the early settlers travelled across America east to west. All good and business as usual.

There I am screaming across the desert in the middle of nowhere. Up ahead, about a mile, there is a little shack at the bottom of an outcrop of rock. As I'm approaching at close to 2 miles a minute (my Dad was a fighter pilot and it rubs off on you) this weird little dude bursts out of the shack and waves his arms at me to slow down. He points right at me and I get this burning feeling in the middle of my forehead. (That's where your third eye is. Go Google!) Old me thinks he's heard the car and wants to sell me a dream-catcher or a necklace. Dumb tourist keeps going.

But that isn't the case. He'd sensed me coming and knew he could help me at exactly the point I needed it even though I didn't realize it at the time. I kept going and thought about the spirit guide I'd had for years who was this giant of a man. A North American Indian. And a Cherokee in Santa Monica had told me this would happen for sixty bucks and my Jimi Hendrix t-shirt two years earlier but I only remembered 50 miles further on. Big mistake. Note to self to switch to receive and come off transmit. Idiot. Big fat idiot. Ignore the Universe at your peril.

11th November 2007

I have just met someone who I know is going to be a big influence on me. Ladies and gentlemen, may I introduce Dr Angela Watkins PhD? I am (finally Mum – see I did it?) at the College of Psychic Studies in London.

Funnily enough, I am immediately struck by how it feels and even smells like my Mum's house. We used to recite that rhyme about the little old woman who lived in a shoe - so her! - and this is how it feels. Green carpet, lots of pink and purple quartz (ever noticed how energizing it is to stand near a big lump of crystal?), tinkling running water and lavender. I'm sitting as a guest in a semi-circle of about 15 women and one other man with a beard. How surprising. The beard I mean. Weird beards. Makes me suspicious. Pipes, sandals and socks or beards. Never trust any of them!

I have never been in something like this and it feels strange yet immediately familiar. I make a sort of quantum leap in understanding at that moment. Angela has our attention. She is lovely, lovely, lovely and makes my heart sing with happiness. I've found another Mummy. Stop that, it's unhealthy and disappointing. A psychologist called William Romeyn once told me that no man truly becomes an adult until his Mother dies and releases him. I admit, I'm still crying inwardly like a weakling about her leaving and have no vision of when that will end. Angela is a fantastic medium, healer and teacher though. Wow. This group of women seem to be a bit needy and unstable quite honestly.

But who am I to judge? I am unstable too. Unpredictable even. Prone to mood swings of Biblical proportions. Not averse to a bit of figurative head chucking over the ramparts. By the way – can I apologise now if you were thinking this book was going to be a nice cosy bit of New Age self-help? It's not. You may even finish it feeling quite disturbed and outside your comfort zone. But you will know something about who we are and what we're for which you didn't before so please persevere. That's the amazing thing about the way collective conscious and the Universe works. I sense you are starting to wonder where this is leading.

Well how do you think I am feeling sitting amongst this group of crazy women? Loving it actually. I can feel a traffic warden giving my bike a ticket outside. Only I could get a parking ticket for a motorbike but I am so captivated I can't move. Actually I can't move because the metal chair I am sitting on has bent under my considerable I was going to say auric field but it's possibly more to do with my 18 stone density to be more accurate. I am a warrior psychic, just like my Mum actually, but maybe they don't get that many Sumo wrestlers turning up for Angela's classes. I tend to just physically punch right though an obstacle which is all wrong. You are supposed to dissolve the obstacle and walk through unimpeded in peace saying Om Shanti or something. Bollocks to that.

The aura which proved too heavy for the chair at my first class with Angela Watkins. This was taken with an aura camera. Everybody's aura is different. It's fun. The bottom area is my creativity and the light above me is my psychic spiritual self. The second shot was taken two years later. I've developed a second creative area and a structure and change section.

I feel sure I can flatten anything which gets in my way. This is wrong I know and is Old Me talking but old habits die hard. What Angela shows us, and the little mediumship practice I am allowed, is cool. I want to definitely know more but am afraid to ask. I have a problem with belonging to clubs. I got stuck in boarding school when I was six and have developed a phobia about anything institutionalised. Especially as I am quite seriously worried I will end up in one, dribbling in a straitjacket. Admit it – how many 16 year olds do you know have had an ECG and electric shock treatment?

They actually used to do that to people like us in those days before they'd heard of crystal and indigo children or Steiner schools. I feel I was perhaps one of the first crystal children pre 1987 Harmonic Convergence. We were seen as anomalies, not the future, as society was struggling to keep up with the rate of evolutionary change which is increasing as the Maya predicted.

The Maya saw it coming and charted it in the Mesoamerican Long Count Calendar 5125 years ago come 2012. They divided it into nine Baktouns as the Nine Ages of Man which consisted of shorter and shorter periods as the speed of things increased, the last and shortest starting in 1776, the Year of Independence. Clever stuff, huh? How could they have known about that? I'll come back to the Maya later. It's important.

Start your own research now – you need to know this to help understand the rhythm of our lives. I am given a small French lady called Suzanne Michal to pair with and I tell her she is a Sea Otter. Turns out she loves Sea Otters. Funny that. In a few years we will be bonded by our personal connection to the tragic Haitian earthquake.

I leave the College of Psychic Studies with my friend Sue Llewellyn. Sue is tall and has a deep brown voice and is a powerful witch in my book. I pluck the ticket off my motorbike and try to dematerialize it which doesn't work. Where are your wizard powers when you really need them?

Dr Angela Watkins, PhD. The most amazing medium, healer and teacher I have ever met and my mentor. Note the little friends by her left arm.

26th December 2007

Boxing Day. I am feeding a friend's cat. She is black and a spirit guide. The cat, not the owner. I like cats. I like animals a lot apart from North American Badgers. Never, ever get near one. They are very bad tempered and they bite. Oh, and tarantulas. They chase you if they feel you stomping about and will bite you if they can.

Come to think of it, there are lots of things out there waiting to bite you. But those two I would single out from the animals I have encountered or filmed close up as ones to avoid. The cat is purring and insinuating itself around my wellies.

My phone rings. It's Angela, although I've temporarily forgotten who she is. The greatest medium I am ever going to meet and I don't recognise her. It's the cat's fault, she is blocking me because of her selfish desire to possess me. Angela asks if I'd like to start attending her mediumship development workshops at her house. I know I would and I accept eagerly, flustered. I'm flustered because I'm worrying what my wife will make of it. My sense is she is finding my increasing interest in the psychic and spiritual alienating.

Back to that Albert Camus scenario on my Mum's deathbed. Alienation is the name of the game. Existentialist alienation. Would my wife leave me? No that is the one thing which would never, ever happen. She doesn't hug me like she used to. But she would never leave me would she? She promised. I close my mind to that ever happening to defend my fragile confidence. Maybe she will love me more if I develop more of a feminine power. I think my soul is a woman anyway. Does that make us lesbians?

5th January 2008

My wife has bought me some lovely books on orbs so maybe she is more supportive than I think. One on the Angel System describes each angel, the colours they appear as and their particular powers. This is amazing. What's even more amazing is I already know most of this. Did my Mum instill it in me so young I don't remember? Did the angels who visited me in my cot tell me? My sense is they might have. The orb pictures I will take more and more of feature white, pink, yellow, green and orange orbs. Archangels Uriel, Chamuel (love), Yellow and fringed with red (Metatron aka Enoch or Elijah as his incarnated self), Raphael and Gabriel.

My wife is supporting me on my journey. Jack has been born now. In fact he's in school and is still being followed around by a giant orb of protection. My sense is it's his Granny looking out for him. I read Noel Edmonds has the same experience and has his Mum and Dad on either shoulder.

Jack accompanied by his Angels of Protection as usual. I'm showing you multiple pictures to demonstrate how consistent orbs are. (Picture courtesy Andrea Boardman)

5th May 2008

Location TV directing work is intense at the moment. My wife and I travel to Kenya for me to research a shoot on disappearing wildlife for a documentary I am going to direct. What a beautiful country. We travel out on a Safari at sundown into the Mara and it is The Lion King for real. A mass of different species move across the grassland as the sun sets. The variety is ridiculous. Giraffe, antelope, zebra, a buffalo (slightly scary animal but at least it doesn't bite), hundreds of different birds, elephant.

My wife isn't well and I notice later there is a tiny orb shadowing her. They are the first pictures I've taken with my new camera and they are appearing on it too. Must be broken like the last one then! This will be followed for me by Engineering Connections with Richard Hammond – there's a man who has an abundance of protection. That accident so nearly killed him – then it's onto Into The West hosted by naturist Jeff Corwin and Ways To Save The Planet.

Richard Hammond, a year after the accident which nearly killed him, presenting my show on engineering.

I spend months in the US filming whales, mountain lions, wolves, rattlers and vinegar beetles with my friends cameraman Glenn Evans from LA, who is a psychic five year old like me, and Jonah Torreano from New York. Jonah is a cynical, laconic multi-talented one off. I love them both like brothers. Still do. We have adventures you can only begin to imagine. And Glenn - I am sorry about almost dropping you down the volcano on Mount Baker from the chopper. I'm spending a lot of time away and so is my wife.

This is often how we roll on location shoots. Planes become buses and it's a battle between distance, cost, speed, schedule and how much stuff we have. This was somewhere in Montana. General Missy is counting bags.

My buddies, soundman and multi-talented dood Jonah Torreano and director of photography Glenn Evans when we were filming in the Grand Canyon, Arizona, with tv naturist host Jeff Corwin.

They might look like a book cover but they were charging us at the time.

39

8th July 2008

Time to talk to you about Angela Watkins again.

I'm at my first mediumship development class at her house in bucolic Wimbledon. Funny word that, bucolic. Sounds like a nasty cough or contraction but it means leafy and green. I have developed an immediate Oedipal crush on her which is both shameful and distracting. Angela is 60 plus and very pretty. She looks you in the eye and deep into your soul. It's not an uncomfortable feeling. Reassuring in fact. I am amongst friends. Like minded. Misfits if I'm honest. As I am. I have felt an outsider my entire life. As if my shoes are on the wrong feet.

I am about to have a series of experiences which are both new and very familiar on a subconscious level. Angela's little house is like a pure portal. It is almost completely white. There are no electronics and it is calm and clear. Even her Scotty dog is white. She lies on my feet a lot. The house reminds me of the wardrobe in "The Lion, The Witch and The Wardrobe". It immediately feels like something which spirits can pass through, hence the portal status.

We are led out in the garden and sprayed with de-clutter spray. She shows us an exercise to clear trapped negative energy from our chakras. I can see snakes of black coiled round one or two spinal columns and I itch to remove it but I am the novice, newly arrived, so I don't dare. My feet feel like the roots of a tree.

We are shown how to ground ourselves. This is the most important exercise for anyone. I can feel my Mum floating around, watching over proceedings. She is happy I have found Angela or is it the other way round? Angela senses her too and tells me which is a little startling. Her eyes shine with a knowing. You wouldn't imagine mediumship could be taught like Spanish classes. It can't quite as you need to be sensitive and to have an open heart and if you have, that's a great start.

We open our chakras including the trap door, as I call it, in the right brain hemisphere. As I visualize it opening I see a bridge and an Angel waiting. He is smiling. He is Metatron and I recognise him as an old friend. He is the keeper of the bridge between life and death. The link between the worlds. The Stellar Gateway.

The Greeks had Hades and the Ancient Egyptians had Osiris. They link to the Underworld but in our culture it's straight to Heaven. No need to row across the Stygian waters with the Grim Reaper. My sense is they are each other's Nemesis. Diametrically opposed and not different interpretations of the same entity. Could be a punch up coming. A chunky five year old with

40

Osiris in one hand and Metatron in the other. Bang! Crash! Power Ranger of the Gods! Who will be victorious?

Watch out, here come their big brothers Set and Sandalphon. These guardians of the door between the worlds have twins: Hades has Zeus (he even has a three headed dog called Cerberus), Metatron has Sandalphon, Osiris was not strictly speaking the brother of Set (a bad god) but Set and Anubis the jackal god were linked. All these twins. Is God a twin?

Makes sense to me but then I am a Gemini myself. God has a male and feminine side. Yin and yang. Black and white. The Divine feminine even has a name, the Shekinah (pronounced like vagina). Set I feel was one of what I call the Dracos or Draconians. Or a Nephilim. I have bad dreams about these things which appear like the monster from Alien. Sort of a giant preying mantis. It's no coincidence the Alien monster struck a primeval fear in us and made the franchise so successful. It's something which was dredged out of our ancient memory, our past life DNA. It's something which used to terrorise us for real. I dare you to Google "Abaddon". He's the beast of the pit and is the ultimate boogieman.

Anyway, this is getting off the point. See? That's why being grounded is so important. It's going to take me a year to set my ego aside so I can channel spirits more effectively. Sounds simple but is the hardest thing to quiet your own ego and let the curtains in the back of your head open so spirits can come through. The first thing I learn about this is you have no jurisdiction on who shows up. Soon I have had two dead twins killed in a car crash, a feisty boxer who ran a Victorian pub and a cat. But channeling the dead is not really my thing. I find it a bit boring. Channelling angels and spirit guides feels more exciting, and connected to my purpose.

41

Angela Watkins's mediumship development class in action. The orbs are mainly between the Sea Otter (Suzanne Michal) and Pauline Davenport sitting on the right.

11th November 2008

So here's what I've learnt so far. I am not cut out to tell grieving people about their dead relatives. In all honesty, they seem to know and aren't that interested in me either. I do love to heal people though and, like my Mum, I have a powerful natural ability for this. I feel we are aliens who have become human and regressed. We have somehow unlearned our natural, innate skills for healing, sensing, communication, seeing and travelling without leaving our present location. I feel the birth of modern science and the industrial revolution have contributed mightily to this. Science and Spirit have been separated. Divide and rule.

Consign what you can't control which might hurt you to myth, demonise it, scare the populous into submission. Paint a black picture about hell and damnation, retribution, forgiveness, sin, enslavement. Demonise the feminine. Call Mary Magdalene a whore. I hate what has happened to us. The message I am getting is it is time to remember who we are. Because time is running out before we have to be sure where we stand and understand the situation. It is no longer good enough to be blind, to dismiss what is about to happen with a non-committal shrug. We are approaching a sharp right turn. If you can, read Revelations at the end of the New Testament.

And I believe the Nephilim are behind some of it. Their existence and their contribution could account for the inexplicable acceleration in our evolution, and the introduction of complex sciences like astro-physics and astronomy amongst ancient races like the Mesopotamians, the Egyptians, the Maya and the Incas.

Imagine Revelations is talking to us in the present. It was actually written about the downfall of the Roman Empire but I think Empires have a similar imprint and cycle. You have to decide what you believe in, what you know. I have also been told some slightly scary things about myself and my purpose. I am directly connected to the ark of the covenant, to the staff of Aaron which is said to be inside the ark along with the ten commandments God gave to Moses. The ark led the Israelites into battle against the Pharisees.

It was captured eventually by the Pharisees but it heralded so much bad luck for them they insisted on giving it back. I believe I am the incarnation of an angel. I believe I am a weapon like the ark and am connected directly to its power. It is hidden through a wormhole which is accessed on Glastonbury Tor and I should go there.

I am a soul rescuer, an exorcist, a sorcerer, and Merlin in a previous incarnation. I am connected to St Germain and the Purple Flame of the Seventh Ray. St Germain was thought to have incarnated as Merlin who helped form the Knights Templar as well as being in the court of King Arthur, with Lady Guinevere (Arthur's missus) and the Knights Of The Round Table.

Phew. That is a lot to lay claim to but there we are.

I am told all or part of this on different occasions by several people who have no knowledge of each other and receive no prompting from me. My life is becoming increasingly surreal. But I feel this is true. I know every weird beard in Christendom is convinced they are half a book's worth of ancient curios from previous incarnations but this is what I am told and it really, really resonates with me. It's the consistency which is interesting. Maybe they say the same things to everyone? My wife thinks I am gullible and overly receptive and maybe she is right. But I know the truth in my heart.

Angela's classes are progressing well and I can feel my psychic sensitivity increasing with focused practice. Unfortunately it also means I can feel my personal life becoming more broken and less solid. And the radio receiver in my head is growing louder and affects me more. Externally it appears as if I am becoming more bi-polar but I know the real reason. But then nutters always claim that don't they? If you ask a full-blown crazy person if they are sane they will look at you as if they are offended you have even dared question their sanity. I know, I've found myself doing it.

Conversely, the effect of this knowing is so pervasive it does sometimes flip over into self-doubt and I start to question it and worry that I am displaying the classic symptoms of paranoid schizophrenia. I feel dizzy and unwell just trying to write this now. My head is expanding and contracting like a lung and my stomach is churning. I have to keep going. Keep talking to you. But it's happening right now, as I'm putting this down for you to read. It feels like long fingers are reaching into my brain and tinkering with it. This isn't anything which is on a higher vibrational level, maybe this is being crazy?

12th November 2008

I'm going to tell you something now and you can make up your own mind. I'm just going to tell you what happened last night. After feeling like I was actually going crazy finally, which might actually have been a migraine as I was violently sick and had to go to bed, I fell asleep and had a dream. One of the preying mantis creatures, all seven feet tall of it, a Nephilim or a Draco, came into my room in my dream and sawed off the front of my skull with a fine surgical saw. I am paralysed in my dream and can only observe what is happening, helpless to do anything.

The creature, which has fine, delicate surgeon's hands, slices off my frontal lobe and lifts that out like a dismantled car engine. It places a large black sac like a breast implant in my brain then puts everything back in place. When I wake up I feel wonderful. Really wonderful. Calm. As if I have had a shot of morphine – something I grew a little too fond of when my bottom disc in my back exploded into my spinal column and when my foot ended up pointing backwards after a bike accident. Hmmm. Happy happy happy.

This is good. I go to the window in the bathroom and look out on a shiny world. Birds are singing. But I feel nothing. Someone has switched off the radio in my head. But I do like the feeling. I'm contained. I feel normal, ordinary. I could really get to like this. Try your crystal dowser says a voice. I take it out and hold the beautiful little quartz dowsing crystal over my left palm with it suspended on its fine silver chain between my right thumb and forefinger as usual.

When I ask it a question it always swings clockwise for yes, anti-clockwise for no. Always. Nothing. No movement whatsoever. So they've found me and got at me. I've been switched off. To stop me finding out. To stop me from writing this book. From sharing what I am learning with you.

But do I mind that much right now? Really? Like on the occasions when I have nearly died I can feel myself slipping towards the goo of complacency which is one step away from death and the Stellar Gateway. I'm not going to die but the feeling that my emotions are not my own, my life is not my own, my future is not mine to determine, will go away if I can just stay in this new blissful state. I could be like everyone else on the terraces, shouting my head off on a Saturday afternoon at a football match while I look forward to a hearty tea and a cuddle with the wife, maybe some kissing, nothing else imposing on my consciousness.

No urging to look to the End of Days, or shooting out into space millions of miles from earth, feeling a trapped soul pass through me on the stairs in someone else's house, no eyes watching me. Shit, some privacy at last. I go upstairs and sit on the side of the bed and stare at the wall which is usually not a wall but a step to somewhere else. Except today it isn't a portal, it's a wall. Almost grudgingly, I force myself to call my friend to help me.

As she talks to me I lie back on the pillows and my neck and head go into a spasm like I have never experienced in my life. It really, really hurts. We visualize taking my brain apart and she can see the black device the mantis/Draco/Nephilim, or whatever it was, planted there in my dream. We remove it and reassemble my brain, figuratively speaking. The pain has gone and the chattering radio is slowly increasing in volume. The familiar shaky nervousness is back. I'm not selling this to myself very well. I hate it. But it's my burden, my destiny, the point of it.

1st December 2008

I am at my worst when I feel someone is hiding something from me because it always means they are going to abandon me and don't want to tell me.

Then I look into them and I know and wish I didn't. I miss my Mum so much. She would never ever lie to me. I knew what she said was the truth and sometimes it hurt to hear it but it was the truth. My wife is the loveliest person I have ever met. She said she would get a gun and shoot me if I was ever unfaithful which I paid attention to but that part was easy anyway as she was all I needed. She gave me everything and I wanted for nothing but that has changed so subtly I haven't even noticed. I trust her so much I have no need to look into her.

11th December 2008

A business trip to Kosovo. I've wanted to visit this tiny country ever since it was dragged into the world headlines in 1995 in the Bosnian war. It wasn't even a country in its own right then and has only just been recognized as such by the UN. I sense this is going to be more than just a business trip. My partners Iain King, an ex army helicopter pilot, and Avni Istrefi, who is Kosovan, are with me. As soon as we touch down I can feel the history of the place. Forces have washed to and fro over it many times.

Curious trapped souls are checking me out as much as I am them. I am walking through Mitrovica, Avni's home town, as he describes how the Serbs sealed up the school he went to and gassed everyone inside. Around 1,000 children and teachers died. We walk on to the bridge over the river which divides the Kosovan and Serb populated parts of the town. The Serbs are still in residence 10 years on from the war. I take a picture and there are faint orbs in the foreground on the bridge. A French KFOR guard asks us to leave the bridge.

He is worried we might be picked off by a Serb sniper who very occasionally takes pot shots at the Kosovans on the opposite river bank. Two children playing there a couple of years earlier were shot. We leave.

Avni shows me a memorial statue of the leader of the Kosovan Liberation Army. He led the Kosovan resistance against the invading Serbs as they came through the mountain pass behind Mitrovica. He was killed in hand to hand combat against the Serbs who were supported by tanks. He died with 27 bullets in his body. He was Avni's elder brother.

Kosovans are the most extraordinary people. Resourceful, industrious, totally trustworthy. Avni is no exception to this. He is a very handsome, quietly spoken man who is always quick to smile and laugh. He has a hug like a car compacter and I have banned him from hugging me as he always puts my neck out.

High fives work fine for me. He has a right fist like a hammer when necessary but is the most artful pourer of oil on troubled waters I have ever seen. Why he isn't Kosovo's Ambassador to the UN is beyond me. His brothers Sami and Bedri work in government already so it is probably only a matter of time. If my family's lives were ever threatened, Avni would be my go to guy.

He takes a picture of me in front of the statue of his brother and it is awash with orbs. I can feel the spirits around me as I pose for the picture. There is even a strange sort of ectoplasm above my head. This land has many spirits still walking the ground where they fell. We go for a haircut and a shave with the old boys who work in the barber's shop in the centre of Mitrovica. They are hilarious and treat us like visiting Royalty. As Iain and I are strolling round the market I take a few quick tourist snaps of the stalls. As we look at the pictures we can both see that one has a blue hexagonal orb in the centre as well as some other blurs and blobs. Later we learn we are standing 50 feet from a mosque where the locals were rounded up.

46

The men and children were shot and the women raped before also being shot. The hexagonal orb is to appear in my pictures repeatedly, across the world. My sense is it is a combination of the presence of Michael and Uriel watching over me and other sensitives will echo my feeling. The hexagonal shape is interesting.

Diana Cooper and Klaus Heinemann (I'll explain who they both are in a bit) say they think they appear as hexagonal because the angel is radiating energy, instead of resting. My sceptical colleagues dismiss it as the effect of the shutter which on a single lens reflex camera is still sometimes mechanical and is hexagonal when almost closed. But that doesn't apply to a compact digital camera like mine which is electronic. It's either on or off. I will show this picture to Stephen Fry a few years later over dinner.

Stephen is a brilliant mind and hugely well-informed but seems to loathe, really loathe, what he sees as conjecture. He becomes incensed with my premise and keeps saying he wasn't there when the photograph, or any of the others I show him, was taken, so how can he possibly comment? I can't recall inviting him to comment - I just wanted to show him and pique his interest.

I thought he would make the perfect host for my TV series on the subject. His angry reaction really surprises me as I have him pegged as an open-minded, well-travelled and inquiring soul. It doesn't end well and I feel my healing self reaching out to him. I know the exorcist who was asked by the couple who bought Stephen Fry's recently-sold flat to exorcise it as they didn't like the atmosphere and were subject to all sorts of carrying on.

What I would like to know is whether or not Stephen had felt it too and how he reacted if he did? Stephen and Richard Dawkins would make for an interesting dinner. They would be queuing up to drive in the nails and light the fire around my feet. This must be how the Spanish Inquisition started.

Archangel Michael and Archangel Uriel combined in Mitrovica market. Hundreds of Kosovans were murdered by the Serbs fifty feet away in the Mosque during the Balkans War.

A closer view of the Archangels. My business partner Iain was looking over my shoulder as I took these
and was as astounded as I was by what we saw.

A few seconds later in the market and the Archangels have moved so close to the lens they look like a white blur.

At the local barbers in Mitrovica, Kosovo, with my business partners Avni Istrefi (left), me and Iain King (right). Archangel Uriel is floating in front of Iain's cardigan. One of Avni's five brothers, Sami, is in the foreground.

49

One of many memorials to the Kosovan soldiers who fell during the 1992-1995 Balkans War. Avni's father is responsible for the Military Memorials. This one is near where Avni's brother died.

The memorial to Avni's brother who led the KLA against the Serbs. That white thing top left is a very fast moving orb which is leaving a trail while the camera shutter is open. Archangel Uriel is sitting on my left arm. (Picture courtesy Avni Istrefi)

A few seconds later Archangel Metatron's characteristic orange-tinged shape makes an appearance. (Picture courtesy Avni Istrefi)

21st January 2009

Should I take the A303 or the M4 to Glastonbury? Last time I was there I was working in Bristol on DIY SOS with Nick Knowles and I dragged the long-suffering Production Manager there for a visit. It was pleasant but I didn't really get it. I knew I should be there but I had zero idea why. The only reason was my mum had suggested I go as it was my special place. She got that right. So here I am again, driving down to Glastonbury. Somerset and the surrounding area are like nowhere else in the country. They have a particular atmosphere. Spacy but nice. Glastonbury is a magnet for every nutter imaginable.

The deluded, eccentric, gifted, unhappy and lost turn up here and I suppose you could suggest that includes me. I have brought my camera and am going to conduct an experiment. I have booked into the George and Pilgrims, the oldest hotel in the area, if not the country. It's so old Henry VIIII stayed there when he popped in to personally hang the last remaining Anglican Abbott Colin Whiting in 1538 on the Tor.

Henry had done a deal with the Roman Catholic church to convert England to Catholicism and dissolve the monasteries around the country. It was called the Reformation which was a posh way of saying "land grab". It involved

51

torturing "confessions" from the unfortunate monks and nuns that they were in the employ of the devil before being put to death. Torture which was carried out in this hotel. Some things never change do they?

Henry had two big black dogs who were witness to the hanging of the Abbot on the Tor. I am staying in a room named after another church leader - Abbot Selwood. A little voice in my head has suggested I might like to stay up and take some pictures to see if I can capture some orbs to prove their existence to myself. I will quickly clean the lens after each shot to remove the chance of a piece of dust being stuck to the lens. An old hotel in a town like Glastonbury has got to be rich pickings hasn't it?

Right. Well this is pretty interesting. Astonishing even. When I check into the room it's empty obviously but alive with curious souls and energies. I turn in for bed but sleep proves impossible. I'm being looked at. I take some pictures. An empty room, albeit a quaint and interesting one. I turn off the light. I still feel like I'm being stared at. I ask the assembled group if they would like to show themselves instead of just staring. Bloody Nora. Blobs everywhere. Flying in formation, all over my pictures. This is a first for me.

I am consciously taking orb pictures. On purpose. Dozens of them. They come and go. I wipe the lens and one particularly big one which looks like a gravy stain won't go and stays in the same position on the lens. I wipe, try different focal depths, but I can't shake it. Then I forget to wipe the lens and it goes immediately. So that's its way of telling me not to be stupid or doubt they can make themselves visible. But I am going to need to show this to physicists, photographers, camera technicians. Oh yes, I want a second and third opinion.

But to my mind as the person sitting up in the room, sweating nervously, this is incontrovertible. Before I left home I tried some controls (what we scientists refer to as establishing controls on experiments! ☺) I photographed rain, dust from the vacuum bag blown into the air, in mirrored bathrooms. Nothing. Same camera, done during the week before. Nada. The rain looked like rain, the dust like dust and the bathroom reflected the flash.

Now tonight it's like the Blackpool Illuminations. This will infuriate a lot of people who cannot, will not, accept the existence of orbs, angels, spirits, guides, or an intelligence other than our own. Well tough shit pal. I am starting a collection which will eventually run into its thousands and there are hundreds of other people who are having the same experience.

Even when sceptics can see the orb they insist on disregarding this phenomenon as a fault or dust. Funnily enough, every time I ask a sceptic for an example of dust on their shots to illustrate their point they can't supply me with even one example. That's because they don't take pictures like I do.

Their minds are closed and the angels can't see you clearly when your light is off. So they don't get any. Which is the point isn't it? Come on, let's evolve as a species a little! Or maybe that should be rewind to the point where the light went out.

3.10 am at the George and Pilgrims Hotel, Glastonbury 22nd January 2009. The first time orbs have appeared on request for me. This experience was so astounding that I couldn't sleep for three days afterwards. Can you feel the energy in this picture? It makes me shiver whenever I look at it.

Taken on a subsequent visit in a different room in the same hotel about a year later. Daylight outside but the Angels are still crowding around including Chamuel and Michael. Omnipresence is an amazing trick.

22nd January 2009

I go up on the Tor the next day to give thanks mainly for the amazing visitation and I am greeted by two big black dogs like the ones Henry VIII was supposed to have had. That is a bit strange. I take a picture of the Tor and it seems to be sitting under two massive orbs. They remind me of the orbs of protection in Yosemite. I didn't know this but guess which saint the Tor is officially dedicated to? Michael. The Protector. I love being near the Tor and it seems to love me back. I leave very happy indeed.

Two black dogs like Henry VIII's on Glastonbury Tor just to make me feel at home.

Glastonbury Tor with two huge orbs of protection. The characteristic red and gold edging suggest they are Archangel Metatron and his twin Archangel Sandalphon.

12th February 2009

I have Klaus Heinemann, an experimental physicist late of Stanford University, to thank for today's diary entry. Heinemann wrote a book called The Orb Project where he applied his considerable quantum physics knowledge to the question of why this phenomenon is becoming so prevalent.

He cites luminosity and the construction of modern digital compact cameras as contributory factors.

First, luminosity. When a neon tube is charged with an electrical current, it excites the molecules of the gas in the tube and they radiate light because they change energy to light. It's the same reason the northern lights glow with that eerie radiance near the poles. Solar energy charged particles (not quite the same as the electricity in the neon tube but charged particles nonetheless) bombard the atmosphere and it makes the gases in the upper atmosphere glow as energy is converted to light. Radio waves are also a form of light. If the visible spectrum was a keyboard, the light we can see would take up then length of a keyboard, the frequencies we can't see with the naked eye would reach all the way to the sun.

Even a Scotsman called John Tyndall used visible lumonosity for the world's first global warming demo in the 19th century when he showed how carbon dioxide traps heat. Heinemann's theory is when we use a flash or the sunlight is particularly strong, the orbs are able to appear in the visible spectrum for a split second and this is when the camera shutter is open. The light charges their molecules or whatever they are made of (no one has been able to study their physical properties yet) and they radiate the energy back as light.

The other key factor is compact cameras are fitted with an infra red light intensifier to improve low light sharpness and reduce picture noise or grain. This accidentally helps record orbs as they are in the longer light wave end of the spectrum, ie the red end where infra red radiation resides. You can capture them on infra red video cameras with ease. Wonder who was at work in the background helping with the development of the compact camera and infra-red photography? How much subtle help do you think we receive from God's Angels and Elders? Why did the human genome inexplicably suddenly accelerate in a straight line of determined evolution like no other species?

OK science lesson over. I'm lying in bed back at home and I can't sleep. Right now I am so excited. My life just changed for good, I can feel it. There's no going back. I am a fully paid up orb photographer. I can't believe the pictures. My wife smiled and said something like "Nice." Huh? Surely this proves there is some sort of presence apart from ours?

That angels do exist, that we are not alone. That something is looking after us. That I will never be abandoned again. That precious "mythology" which has been buried under a smug landslide of science is in fact real. Who has been trying so hard to bury it? Not the team who were kicked out of heaven by Michael, Sandalphon and Enoch surely? I am talking about the Devil's posse. Is science their revenge on us for discarding them? Science was invented to bury who we really are not discover it. I believe in evolution – how can you possibly not? – but we seem less enlightened than we were 200 years ago not more.

I do have mixed feelings. I am fascinated by science and I love it but maybe it is the work of the Devil! Sorry Richard Dawkins – this will all infuriate you. I sound like a wizened old crone from Macbeth don't I? But science totally runs our lives now. And what if a massive solar storm in the future wipes out comms satellites, power, GPS, computers, and power stations? (Which it will. It happens on a smaller scale quite often.) A really big belch of cosmic rays from the sun like the one 14,000 years ago could bring the planet to a halt. Wipe out a lot of life. Did you know that?

14th February 2009

I've just read some of Diana Cooper's books on orbs and unicorns. I feel I know her from somewhere. I want to have contact with her so I have written Diana an email to compare notes. Astonishingly, this revered author and public speaker is on the phone. She wants to meet. She feels we are both from the same planet, literally. Sirius B in this case. One more crazy-sounding theory to add to the pile. How exciting is that? And why me? I know she gets thousands of emails. But I was thinking.

If you knew nothing about yourself, if you had a nasty bout of amnesia, you would want to piece it altogether wouldn't you? And I am starting to have huge, very generous clumps of information given to me. They want me to wake up and tell others these new facts of life. New order. Great band.

I'm becoming increasingly aware of a sort of mental padlock on my third eye. In my forehead. I am receiving information which I can't decode. I certainly can't understand much of what I am discovering or being told. There are things which resonate immediately and other information which is already there and I know but I feel as if I am somehow absorbing far more than I realise and it is being stored.

18th February 2009

I am driving through the gates of Diana Cooper's property. It is called Kumeka House. After a spiritual deity called Lord Kumeka. He is Diana's guide and, she claims, the source of inspiration for some of her books. This should be an interesting meeting. Diana is a world-famous source of inspiration for believers in orbs, angels, spirits, pixies, elves, unicorns, esaks and all manner of wonderful things in Heaven and earth. She comes out to meet me and is just as lovely as her books.

But boy, I thought I was harbouring some outlandish ideas. Diana is a very advanced being indeed. I look into her eyes and feel only sincerity and conviction. She is just the kindest person you could ever hope to meet. She says she felt immediately with me that I was an Atlantean like her and that our souls had both originated from other planets. She does look very familiar somehow, I'll give her that. My sense is that what she is telling me is true.

Sorry Richard Dawkins – I have nothing to base it on apart from my gut feeling and the feeling there are a group of angels around us nodding happily. And do you know what? It is so liberating. I choose to believe, to feel comfortable with the extraordinary journey she is taking me on. I don't want to put her on the spot, cross-examine her, shoot her down in flames. I want to bathe in the positive, to have hope, to believe there is something better.

Try this: spend a day questioning everything you hear or read. Have a news channel on all day. Question the point of your own existence. Question your relationships. Your future. Then see how unhappy and discontent you feel. That's a typical day for lots of us, including me. Then try this: spend a day where you don't read a newspaper or listen to the news. Don't question everything. Just allow yourself the luxury of believing in good. Give yourself a hug and congratulate yourself on being an amazing thing.

Tell yourself you like *you*. I didn't do this until my wife suggested it when I was 50 years old. I sat for half an hour with my jaw dangling around while it sunk in. It's why the bad guys have the planet in their thrall at the moment. We are in the grip of negativity, fear and hatred so much that we have forgotten to love ourselves. Has to change.

Diana, with her fascinating ideas and unique talents, is a lovely example of the power of the positive. She is an angel like my Mum and Angela. It's so easy to dismiss and ridicule the simple truth incarnated angels offer you. All you need to do is take it to your heart. And that takes a courage these days which shouldn't be necessary but it is.

I can confess I am crying right now. This is such a beautiful truth. I cry a lot. I can't help it but I have started to do it more as I feel things more and more powerfully. We are not alone. I was worried we might be out here in the frozen silent vacuum of space. But love is a universal, powerful truth. Crikey – I need a tree to hug. Give yourself permission to have a little cry. Feel what that feels like. Hug whoever is nearest. Right now. Even if he's selling the Big Issue or smells of urine. He needs it as much as you do. More.

This is the effect Diana has. And that has to be a good thing. So why do we instinctively want to make an example of the pure of heart? Kill them? Burn them? Nail them to a cross? Torture them to confess some abomination? Because we are frightened of the transcendental power of love, that's why.

Women seem to have it in greater quantities than men. Probably why men portray women as evil temptresses like Eve, Lilith, Jezebel and Mary Magdalene. Men still try to control women. I am unhappy about this fact. My soul is the Shekinah, the Divine Feminine.

Diana Cooper, author and public speaker on the Angelic Realm and many other things, at home in her meditation room.

28th February 2009

My monthly mediumship development sessions with Angela are going from strength to strength. She is a marvelous, funny teacher. If I'm honest, it's a multi-Mum love fest for me. There is a range of ages and abilities amongst the people who attend regularly but it is comforting to be amongst others who are like me and remind me to varying degrees of Mum. I am still missing her terribly. You shouldn't underestimate how debilitating loss is. I feel her loss every day. To my surprise I expected to feel her near but I don't. It's as if she has gone a very long way away. Maybe back to Sirius?

Look - while you are giggling about this idea, consider the fact that we only discovered Chiron recently. A whole planet skulking around on the fringes of our own solar system. We've had telescopes for 200 years but it took a really sensitive one to spot it. It had been there the whole time but we only just found it. Which doesn't mean it wasn't there before. See how we instinctively trust science?

If scientists tell us something, it must be true. They have told us Chiron exists so we believe them. Have you ever seen it yourself? We have become believers in the church of science. Maybe that's why the west is experiencing a slow decline into aetheism while the middle east and Africa is increasing the conviction of its beliefs and its embrace of Islam. Same God, vastly different theology and hence motivation.

Something very odd happened in the class today. I have dreamt in a funny language occasionally since I was little and today when we are sitting in a circle taking it in turns to try inspirational speaking, I can feel a small group of beings standing behind me. One of them steps forward and sits *into* me, which is bloody odd I can tell you. I sort of mentally step aside and watch from a few feet away. My arms are rising up in the air. I look ridiculous. Then Angela is addressing me and I realise time has passed. She is saying I was speaking in a different language and I had brought too many spirits forward at once. I am shocked and to my embarrassment I start crying.

This is a rather frightening loss of control. But at the same time, it is exciting. Something is in my knowing which wasn't there before is present. I am an ancient being. A shaman. I can conjure these powerful guides forward when I need their help or there is a job to be done. Like the walls of Babylon being blown down or a path through a sea created or a dragon slayed. Draco - Dragon. Latin for dragon isn't it?

The lady who had been sitting next to me, who happens to be a wonderful opera singer despite the fact she is almost totally deaf, says she thought what I was speaking sounded like Aramaic which she has studied. The language of the Israelites in Egypt. The language of Jesus. Wow. And before you say anything, she has got a couple of good hearing aids.

1st March 2009

I'm becoming increasingly interested in shamanism. Every culture has its witch doctors, medicine men, healers, oracles, call them what you like but as with the commonality of the figure who ferries souls across the divide between life and death and is called either Hades, Osiris or Enoch/Metatron, depending on your origins, it's the same box of oranges. I really feel I am something like that.

My experiences keep pointing me back to three or four really powerful, vivid, spirit guides who are around me. The North American Indian seems to have faded slightly but I have a Mongolian spirit, another who is dressed in beautiful feathers and turquoise and is an Aztec or Maya and a Druid connected to Glastonbury.

They have shown themselves to help me with my development as a shaman myself and to protect me against what is coming. Whatever that is. Angela keeps talking about my relationship with the ark of the covenant and a group of protective spirits who she says remind her of Darth Vader. Tiny men with black helmets and black armour made from bamboo and leather. Mini Samurai. All very disconnected and makes little sense to me as yet.

But that is the pattern I am discovering. It always seems obscure til a certain moment when it snaps into stark relief and becomes clear. It's probably because we are just not good enough yet at interpreting the messages and information we are given. The concept of communing with the spirits of ancestors is the basis of belief across Asia from China to Papua New Guinea. Angela says I should visit Glastonbury again and think about finding myself a suitable staff or stick to go with the aura of a shaman I have started to project.

2nd March 2009

A day later, Sunday, I am driving through Turnham Green in Chiswick, London. I am thinking as I drive about how many other people there are out there like me. How many aliens, spawn of the devil, prophets, sons and daughters of God, and angels are currently walking the earth? Taking it as fact for a moment that I am not a normal human, who else is there? How many of them live in Chiswick?

Then I see an Afro-Caribbean man in a sheepherder's duster down to his ankles riding a bike. He has a matching hat on. He is dressed for really bad weather but the sun is shining and it's quite a nice day. And he has a walking stick strapped to the parcel carrier on the back. Not any ordinary stick. It's my staff. My staff.

I draw level with him and swoosh the passenger window down. So he turns as he cycles and sees my face looking at him from the driver's seat. I'm in a black SUV with blacked out windows. (Every shaman has one dontcha know?) I ask him if the stick is for sale. Yes he says. Can I buy it? Yes he

61

says again, quite serenely. I could swear he's cycling in slow motion as he seems to be moving much faster than his legs would suggest. We pull over.

He tells me the history of the – my – stick. It's Kenyan baobub wood. OK, liking this a lot already. It has a warrior's proud face carved in the handle and a triangular bit on the top almost like the Egyptian ankh of Horus. I suddenly have a vision of striking the staff on flagstones and a blue shockwave shooting out around the world. The flagstones are in the Tor. I don't care how much he wants, I'll pay it. I have a load of cash in the car I am planning to pay a bill with so bring it on. £300 at least.

I know it's going to be a lot. You have to be prepared pay for something if it's worth the price. How much? I ask, cutting to the chase. I'm very goal oriented like that. He opens his mouth to speak then smiles at me in a funny way and changes the subject. Oh come on. Let's do a deal! £20 he says. Ah ha. Bargain! What was I saying about love is free? The angels are laughing.

They do have a sense of humour. They really do and they are laughing now. I take my staff and run my hand down its familiar feeling smooth brown shaft. Alright, alright, steady - it's not that kind of book, sorry. Another piece in the puzzle just came together.

The man in the coat was real by the way. He gave me his mobile number and I called it the next day, just to see if he answered and he did. So the question is do angels have mobiles now or he was just a bloke flogging curios? You decide about that one.

My powerful staff, which carries the purple flame of St Germain. I bought it from a very mysterious man in Turnham Green. I think he might have been an Assyrian in a former life.

9th March 2009

I'm going to Glastonbury again. I have my staff and I sort of want to try it out. Today's date feels right for some reason. It's going to be cold up on the Tor. I have decided to try going up there in the dark. On my own. I am scared already

I have also visited Chagford on Exmoor this trip. Only because I liked the sound of the Chagford Triangle which the guys on the Nick Knowles DIY SOS TV show called it as they are from Chagford themselves. I have dinner with myself in the pub/hotel next to the graveyard in Chagford and drink a whole bottle of wine to celebrate my loneliness and general idiocy. The hotel is, suitably enough, called the Globe. My tri-field meter which I use to measure electro magnetic fields, micro wave and electrical shows the EMF in the pub is off the scale. This is sometimes caused by cookers, microwaves or TVs. But it's consistent throughout.

Off. The. Scale.

Something is creating an EMF which shouldn't.

Usually means there is an entity or something attached to the property. I stumble over to the graveyard and hang around taking pictures. I feel quite at home amongst dead people. They like me and I like them. All good. Then I take a picture of some headstones and a bunch or two of daffodils. As a scientific control I take another one of the same frame and the image is full of what looks like smoke. My first thought is my breath might have misted up and caused it so I try breathing out and photographing it.

Nothing. It's too warm and dry. I think I just photographed what the Victorians used to quaintly call ectoplasm. Next morning, the tri-field meter doesn't register anything. Same hotel, same lights and cookers on. Odd. I visit Dartmoor Prison and manage to fall down a drain and bash my face.

Back in Glastonbury I use every excuse I can to put off getting back in the car and driving up to the Tor which I can make out in the darkness as it is faintly illuminated by the moon.

I stop by Chalice Well at the base of the mound which the Tor was built on to fill up a bottle of its iron-rich water from the well. It's been there for a million years and filters water though the sandstone. It's supposed to be good for you and have magic properties but to me it tastes like I imagine the bottom of a kettle would. I'm just no good at this hippy stuff. I start the short climb up the winding steps to the Tor which towers above me. I can almost hear it humming 'come and have a go if you're hard enough'. I am so nervous and twitchy. This is ridiculous. Think of it as home - that might help.

The wind is blowing hard when I reach the Tor and it feels like a different climate to the one at ground level. The wind howls through the open arches of the Tor. Are you there Michael? I'm not sure what I'm supposed to do and there's no one to ask apart from the angels. So I ask them what to do. I find myself striking my staff on the flagstones. Ooh that feels good. Scary, but good. Now what? Think I'll take some pictures.

When in doubt take some pictures. I concentrate on tuning in to the schism between where I am and the dimension where I think the ark is hidden. This idea pops into my head. Did I put it there? Do I hold the key to reach it? I believe I do. That's interesting. I think about the sacred purple flame of St Germain and the seven rays represented by different saints. Gold and violet flames. St Germain...Merlin...the Tor...the sacred flame...me. There is a connection. I sense it is connected.

Maybe that's why I wrote that screenplay about Merlin. Holy crap it's cold up here. And then a small sheet of flame shoots past my right leg. I spin round to see what joker has brought a flame thrower up those steps. There's no one there. I think I was taking a picture with the camera in my left hand just now. I wonder? I check on the viewfinder. Yes, there it is! A bolt of flame with a Y-shaped head. It looks the same shape as the staff in my right hand. My eyes are watering from the freezing cold wind biting into my face.

The flame is where my staff should have been in the picture. Did I just do some full on wizard conjuring? This is like a movie but it really just happened. I am now properly freaked out. I honestly feel I am about to step right through a gateway between here and there. Am I about to be reunited with the ark?

Apart from the keening of the wind, there is nothing. I don't understand what just happened. Time to go. But I think I just got what I would call unequivocal evidence that there is something extraordinary about this place. My Mum was right. It is a portal and there is something happening in my life which is telling me to pay attention.

I took these next two photos eight seconds apart in Chagford Graveyard.

his is quite a common phenomenon but it is freaky when it happens to you! I saw the mist as the flash went but it was gone by the next shot. It's a ghost of some description.

As a comparison, I took this on Glastonbury Tor a few months later than the Chagford picture. There are three distinct faces with the upturned eyes of the Nephilim.

66

I took this a few minutes after the previous shot from the same angle as reference. Angela Davis kindly provides some scale.

This was the first photo I took which made me feel I have a special connection to Glastonbury like my Mum said and that perhaps I have some sort of ability to project energy. That sheet of flame is where my staff should have been in the shot.

16th March 2009

I am staying with my friends Fiona and Bruno. They have a lovely Doberman called Sable who is getting very old now. I'm sorry to say when I see her I know she is going to die. Very sad to see this once muscular, pretty animal so ravaged. I can sense Metatron around her. Technically I suppose he is the angel of death, as he is Gatekeeper of the Stellar Gateway. I take some pictures and it is possible to see Metatron's shadow progressively closing in around her while two orbs of protection sit on her back.

I can sense the love and compassion surrounding this wonderful animal. Sable is scared and paces the kitchen crying. It's a very sad scene and it makes me cry. She knows what's coming and the Angels are comforting her and protecting her. I see Archangel Metatron's shadow drawing across her and it's in the photos. She dies two days later. Bless you Sable, beautiful puppy.

In this next sequence of three photos of Sable Brenninkmeijer, the Angels of Protection are hovering near her back as Archangel Metatron's shadow starts to move across her.

The shadow intensifies as one Angel moves closer to me and appears much bigger while the other stands guard.

Both Angels are diffusing to protect Sable from the intensifying shadow of the Angel Of Death. The right hand side should have the same light value as the left side but is much darker. For me this is one of the most beautiful sequences of photos I have ever taken as I loved Sable so much.

69

20th March 2009

My friend Cherie has been my massage therapist for 15 years. She is descended from North American Indians and she has eyes which look into your soul. We had a conversation a while ago about photographing orbs and the spirit world. She says she has started taking a lot more and she sure has. She is very connected to the spirit world and to our ancestors. Cherie once told me she can recall the times between incarnations as well as her previous lives. That is not something I have ever come across before.

She says there are records of everything which has ever happened in the Akashic record. Every being which has lived, every molecule of our existence. She feels she was an Atlantean and may have come from Sirius like me and Diana. A network of souls is being revealed to me of people like Cherie who have the same sensitivity as I do. There are a lot of us and there is comfort in being with them. My sense of being a misfit is receding slightly. I have also begun to notice that people in general seem to be increasingly more receptive to talking about this sort of thing and are open to possibilities.

The change is marked. We are not as cocky as we were – it's been knocked out of us. Not quite the Masters and Mistresses of the Universe we once thought are we? I am getting the sense that we are being woken up. By something outside ourselves. The arc of my journey has a lot in common with others. I benefit from my science background as I try to keep the amazing experiences I am having in the realm of the scientific, merged with the spiritual.

I am convinced science and higher intelligence or the collective consciousness are linked so much one must be superimposed on the other. For instance, the more I discover about quantum physics, the more of what we think as inexplicable paranormal activity can be explained. Well, the manifestation can be explained.

The reasons are the subject of endless scientific hypothesis which is the nature of the quantum theory. Did you know for instance that the Casimir Effect, named after the Russian scientist who discovered it, found that if something is cooled to as near as dammit absolute zero Kelvin (which is very cold indeed – minus 275 deg C), the molecules it is made from stop moving completely? Molecules jiggle around from something called Brownian Motion but not when they get really cold. And it is thought that the energy of the universe would be released as a result. Sound nuts?

Banging two lumps of radioactive metal together to make your own sun sounds pretty outlandish too – it's called a nuclear weapon. And a scientist called Evgeny Podkletnov – Russian again – found if you supercooled a ceramic plate, then rotated it at 18000 rpm above a bed of magnets it would float on the electro magnetic field. So you have a non-metallic substance floating above magnets which in theory isn't possible. I've seen the NASA footage and spoken to Podkletnov – he's in hiding now, well Norway actually. Both examples go against what we think we know about the way things work. And it's as true in the unseen spiritual world as much as it is in the tangible scientific one.

Cherie can conjure orbs at will like me. There are lots of us who can do this scattered around the world.

25th March 2009

The padlock on my third eye, although figurative, is becoming annoying. So much information has been downloaded to me and I need to know what it says! It feels like a having a zip file in your brain which needs the right password to unpack it. Cherie comes to visit Diana Cooper with me.

Having these two together honestly feel likes a meeting of the Counsel of Elders in Atlanta. The conversation is not of this earth. It begins to feel as if there are dozens of others who are with us. I have this picture in my head of a huge hall full of steeply banked tiers. Tall creatures with smooth oblong heads and almond shaped eyes which lack irises fill the hall.

They wear long brown robes. They are listening to our conversation as the sofas have been transported to the hall and we sit before them as we speak. Then the area around Cherie and Diana starts to recede into a white light. All I can see is them. They are unlocking the padlock. A long stream of hissing, chattering, dancing information sings in my head. The lock is gone.

I think I need a cup of tea. The elbow in our existence shoots toward me where we must change direction collectively. 2012 jumps out and it's not looking particularly good. Is this what all this is about? Are they trying to warn us? No I think prepare us is more accurate.

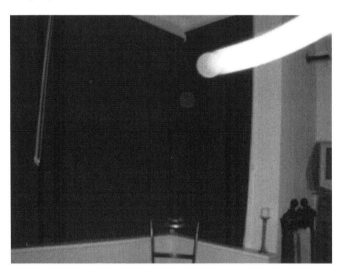

Cherie has hundreds of photos. It was difficult to decide which one to include but I love this one as it illustrates the speed which orbs can move while the shutter is open. It did it again a few seconds later!

26th March 2009

I read Revelations again when I get home. On one level it is a lot of fire and brimstone gobbledeegook which was written 2000 years ago. On another it could apply to us. Is the end of the human race written in to the last book of the New Testament? There are a lot of references to the anti-Christ, loss of hope, the Beast rising out of the Pit. The four horseman of the Apocalypse are a particularly terrifying and modern vision. The one dressed in red? The Pope? He wears red a lot. The Pale Rider?

In my screenplay about Merlin (tragically and unjustly unpublished so far) his Nemesis is called the Pale Man and is a tall, bald albino. Sounds spookily familiar now I think about it. I consider the decade we are currently in. An 800 mile long mountain range 150 feet high appeared off the coast of Indonesia in a few seconds on the floor of the ocean. The resulting shock wave swept the sea into a huge bulge which killed 250,000 people as it piled up the water on the shore. A scar 150 miles long appeared along the base of the Himalayas running left to right across the Hindu Kush in Pakistan, killing at least 60,000 although no one is quite sure of the exact number.

Central China is rocked with a powerful earthquake too. Thousands die including entire schools of children caught in their classrooms. Haiti is to yet to come, as are Chile, New Zealand and Japan. And I have already witnessed Indonesia and Pakistan with my own eyes. How weird is that? I have yet to experience the horror in Haiti and the sight of the entire coastline of southern Chile rising out of the sea ten feet.

It's such a big event, it will affect the speed of the earth's rotation. All in the same decade? What is going on? My sense is it is leading to something. I am being directed to these places to witness it and hold the scale of the destruction in my memory to articulate a warning. No one is going to want to hear this. Thanks guys. They want to hear about abundance and good things instead but maybe we have chanced our luck once too often. No one likes bad news which affects them. They don't mind watching it about other lands far away though – that's more like entertainment.

Watching someone else suffer makes you feel a bit better about your own life, doesn't it? Oh well, I need to look even deeper into my heart and ask for guidance to draw the correct conclusion. Maybe it will be a positive thing which will lift the human race out of its misery and desolation? But you can't make an omelette without breaking some eggs first can you? By the way I met the scientist whose job it was to watch for quakes in the Pacific. But only off the United States. He saw the Indonesian 8.1 and knew it would be bad as the centre was so close to the coast of Indonesia but, and I quote, he "didn't know who to call". They do now.

1st April 2009

Jack, the little boy who had the orb near his mum's tummy when he was in it, is getting bigger, as children seem to do. And in almost every picture anyone takes of him, in particular his mum Andrea who I have known for years and is married to one of my best friends, he is accompanied by some of the biggest orbs you can squeeze into a picture. We feel these are his grandparents. Don't know why we should think that, but we do. It just seems right.

And that is how this instinct works. Things either feel right or they don't. Everyone can understand that but if you are a sensitive, you just know. Even if no one wants to hear it, or it makes you sound bonkers, or it even alienates you from people, you are stuck with knowing the truth about things. Lots of people are more comfortable with tangible evidence, or what scientists tell them, some really irrational people even believe what politicians tell them, but I am learning slowly to trust my intuition, my sense, my knowing. Professionally I have walked out of a meeting many times and said something like they will betray us or I don't like him/her and my colleagues have scoffed and told me to shut up. But I am hardly ever wrong. You can't hide who you are from people like us.

And Jack has some adoring angels of protection around him. They float near him the entire time. He is even pictured reaching up and touching one. I wonder what will happen to him as an adult? Modern children, the last two generations, are referred to as first indigo, then crystal, children. All very New Age and all that, but there is some sense in this.

The Maya foresaw a speeding up in the thirteen ages of man they refer to in the Long Count calendar which started 5125 years ago. They believed we would start to evolve faster and I can see that happening right now. The traditional education system doesn't seem to serve the needs of the children in it. The disconnected, the dreamers, the ones with concentration problems are put on Ritalin. We are sedating a generation of children who are behaving in the way they do because they have leaped forward in their evolutionary development. Why would they not respond to the savage acceleration in the world's heartbeat?

The laptops they balance on their knees contain more computing power than the entire NASA system which put men on the moon. We need to examine what is going on in children's minds with new eyes. They are being born more psychic, more able to connect with the angel network, more receptive. They can hear the voices their parents have shut themselves away from. Just a quick trawl through the photographs of your young friends or your children's own pictures or their young contemporaries will throw up hundreds of pictures of orbs. But the question is why is this happening? Why are children so much more receptive than they used to be?

What are they being readied for? My sense is that something significant is coming and the Angel Realm or the Elders who preside over life are working hard to prepare us, their greatest experiment and manifestation of that is in the Universe. And that something could be our own destruction or spiritual release, or both. I'm just not sure. Back to Revelations where this is discussed in Biblical double-talk. It refers to the Rapture where souls who are ascended spiritually disappear in an instant from the earth when the End of Days comes, leaving others to suffer the blight of the destruction of the world and everything in it. I have an aversion to tub-thumping, fire and brimstone and extremists threatening all manner of nasty endings for sinners, so forget it.

But there is a light bulb on in my head and my heart is beating hard. I'm being told a universal truth with some certainty, but what is it? My sense is we are approaching a cyclical point of change and we need to prepare. Consider this as change: what if we just said no to repression, to fear, to hatred, killing, to war? To the aspects of the human race which bring us down. We must have a choice, surely? This is being used to control people in their billions by their rulers and the hidden rulers above them.

You didn't think it was governments who hold the reins do you? They are told what to do by their masters and it is all about the money, all of the time as my lovely friend Canadian entrepreneur Kevin O'Leary from our Discovery series Ways To Save The Planet likes to say. And the need for control Satan and his consorts crave. Are we about to take a massive leap into the light, away from the grip of Lucifer? Is this what it's about? Is this what they are trying to show me? I feel it might be. And maybe they picked me because I can hear them and because I am not the sort of person who goes through life as if I was presenting Listen With Mother. I call a spade a spade.

Jack at school, with the other kids while his Grandfather Stan entertains them. Can you see the orb of protection which constantly accompanies Jack? Bit hard to miss isn't it? (Pic courtesy Andrea Boardman)

Jack and his Grandfather Stan Boardman at Liverpool FC's memorial room as Jack touches his orb of protection. He seems to know where it is. (Pic courtesy Andrea Boardman)

10th March 2009

I am experiencing an increasing amount of cynicism about my pictures inversely proportional to my own enthusiasm and conviction. It's inevitable I suppose that it should happen. Present anyone with a stimulus or a proposition and they will question it. Fair enough. I did. I do.

Now, here's the thing. People who are naturally receptive and open look at my growing collection of photos of things which shouldn't be there take it on board. The cynical, who are out of reach and shut down, just can't do this. They really can't and it disturbs them that you fail to see why they can't. Trailing round with Diana Cooper and my wife to see commissioning editors about a proposal for a TV series on the subject of orbs is an interesting experience. 30 of them say thanks but no thanks.

We're offering something, supported by pretty strong photographic evidence, that claims to prove we are not alone, that angels exist, that there is an intelligence outside ours, that they are doing their best to reach out to us. And not one of them can find a slot in their packed schedules of fat farms, cookery fests and cop shows for a voice which carries the message so many people would like to hear. At least put it out there and let people think about the idea for themselves. But no, that can't happen. Broadcasters think 'we've got them where we want them. We don't want to disturb the hypnotic slumber. It might cause a revolution. They might not want to buy our advertisers rubbish anymore'.

Everyone is at pains to be civil to us, not to be seen to laugh at these misguided nutters. Maybe they are worried about being turned into a frog or a tent peg? And they express the same viewpoint along the lines of 'I am personally very interested in this idea, but it doesn't fit with what we're looking for at the moment.' Course not. How could it? It's only the most important truth you could tell your audience.

23rd March 2009

Scientist friends are suggesting I buy a stereoscopic camera which takes two slightly different images recorded at exactly the same moment. This apparently will prove that what we are photographing (oh yes, there are lots of us it now seems) is just dust. Not sure I understand this. We are dealing with a celestial intelligence which does what it likes and having the arrogance to we think we can decide when they appear to us, instead of the other way round, just isn't right.

One cynic even says to me that they can't be that clever if all they can do is appear as blobs of light, even if they are sometimes quite beautiful blobs.

Really? I don't see you being able to appear in their domain in any shape or form matey so who's the clever one? This reminds me of the Roman soldiers taunting Jesus when he was said to be on the cross and dying. They challenged him to save himself if he was the son of God. Apparently he did at the end of the movie but not until he had died for our sins.

I'm starting to feel bar room punchy about this as it is starting to annoy me. Bad dose of paradigm blindness. So I have bought a new camera to use alongside my trusty Olympus which I have been using to photograph pictures of orbs running into the hundreds. Just as well they don't seem to appear when I'm working with our expensive broadcast video cameras. The cameramen would kill me if there were little angels whizzing around in the pictures and I'd be out of work! It's another digital camera, a Panasonic EX-7. I take it out of the box and charge it up.

We have a huge roof space on top of the house and I've been up there tonight to road test the new camera. Almost the first picture I take with it records an orb in the corner of the shot the size of a frying pan. Oh no, another broken camera and this one is brand new. Excuse the sarcasm but I've been getting that comment a lot and it is starting to get on my tits.

The first picture I take with my new camera up on the roof at Ashchurch Grove as I'm tired of being told the old one is broken. An orb the size of a frying pan helpfully shows up to prove the point.

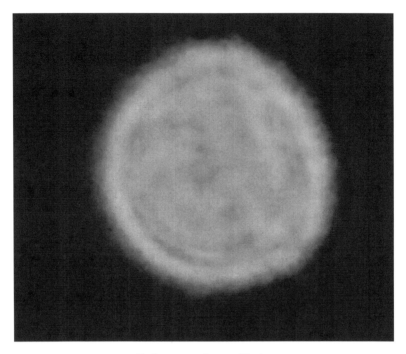

Frying pan orb magnified.

25th April 2009

An old school friend, Jay Stapley, is playing a gig tonight at my favourite pub, the Bull's Head in Barnes. It's an old place and I have found that it is always alive with orbs. They love music and you often see lots at festivals, on the dance floor or at gigs. Jay used to sit next to me in English and play air guitar. He claims to have no recollection of this but I can confirm he did. He would sing the guitar music he could hear in his head.

I like listening to Jay as he has a wealth of experience playing on tour with Pink Floyd and all sorts. I think he's slightly frightened of me. He launches into his set and I start taking pictures. Lots of orbs already. I am getting more attuned to seeing them with my own eyes or sensing where they are. There is a beautiful blue one floating around his head. I sense this is his musical connection to the Divine.

I have always felt that musicians draw their inspiration from a higher source. Mozart is the perfect example of this. His music was the music of God, downloaded through a sensitive musical genius. When Mozart was still in his early twenties he was invited as a special guest to the Vatican to listen to a recital of Allegri's work, the Miserere. In those days, the Vatican commissioned a lot of private works which were forbidden to be performed outside the walls of Vatican City. The Miserere is possibly the most haunting choral work I have ever been exposed to. It's fiendishly complex and full of strange twists and turns in the arrangement of the voices.

Mozart memorized the entire twelve minute piece and wrote it down when he got home after hearing it once and it got out into the world. That is astonishing. Jay is no Mozart but he is a great little electric guitar player. He and I grew up on Jimi Hendrix, Albert King, Albert Lee, John Lee Hooker, Jimmy Isley, Duane Allman, Dicky Betts…delicious. And there it is. The blue orb is drifting across the stage above Jay's head and it is doing something I haven't seen before. It is attached to his head with tiny blue tendrils. It is actually connected to him.

Jay Stapley on guitar, Bulls Head, Barnes, London. Lots of orbs around including the big one at the top of the picture which was floating around.

Surrounded by some familiar angelic forms, Jay's musical inspiration is feeding into his head with blue tendrils from the orb above him.

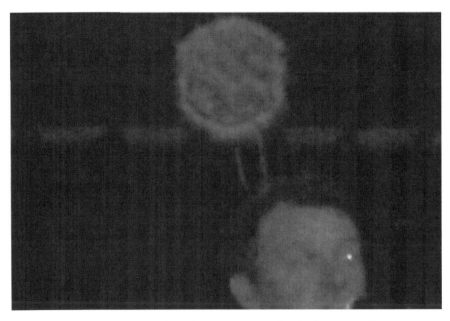

The same picture enlarged so you can see the detail more easily.

21st April 2009

The angels float into me and hug me which is comforting and sustaining. I am humbled by the simplicity and purity of the love I feel. It comes out of nowhere. You can't show people what it looks like. It just is. Beautiful.

I decide to again visit my holy place, Glastonbury, for comfort and possibly some insight. I don't know it yet but I will witness the most extraordinary thing this visit. I stay at my regular landing spot, Meare Manor.

9th September 2009

It is a perfectly still, clear night on the Tor. The moon is bright in the sky. I haven't realized the date: 09/09/09. My life is about to change completely again.

As I walk up the final few steps to the Tor I feel the presence of my Druidic guide. I am raising my vibrational level and opening my chakras, having grounded myself before starting the climb. My Mum always coached me on the importance of grounding. It stops you from floating off untethered. It means you can get back into your body safely at the end of whatever it is you've been up to, when you are channeling, or even confronting the odd entity or demon – and they like to hop into you and hitch a ride if they can.

Then you can start getting ill, or tired, depressed or worse. Grounding. You know it makes sense. Angela Watkins taught me a good visualization of grounding. She says imagine a blue line going out from your base chakra, ie your bum, down into the centre of the earth and winding round an anchor or pole so you are safely tied down.

So I there I am lowering my blue line into the earth down below before starting the climb. My Druid guide asks me to use my Tibetan singing bowl. I have this wonderful friend called Paul Wilkinson at Creative Earth who has singing bowls and all manner of wonderful shamanic equipment. I got my bowl from him, as well as a Mongolian shamanic drum with a beautiful oak handle and a Mongolian shamanic necklace made of Yak's teeth.

The necklace is exceedingly powerful and we feel dates from around the same time as the bowl. The bowl dates back to the 17th century and is wonderful. It is thicker at the lip of the bowl than the base which was a hard thing to do when casting a hand beaten bowl. It makes the bowl resonate louder. It is made from an alloy of bronze, copper, tin and iron like a church bell.

You make it sing by running a wooden stick around its lip like you can do with a wine glass and your finger and the sound it makes is fascinating. It calls in Spirit and raises the vibrational level. The monks would use it at prayers for the same reason. The way the sound oscillates changes from use to use, and from day to day. My mum gave me a small example 20 years ago and I didn't even know what one was then. The sound oscillates with a varying rhythm. Some people love it and it goes right through their pineal gland. Others hate it. I think your reaction is a little bit of a test of your own vibrational level. The higher it is, the better and more positively the individual seems to respond.

I walk around the Tor in a clockwise direction and the bowl rings out its hypnotic call. Under the guidance of the Druid, I perform a cleansing ceremony with my staff and ask for healing, mercy, light and knowing for everyone. I bang the stick on the flagstones and visualize a dark blue energy field being emitted from the base of the stick, out and away from the Tor around the world. I breathe in, my head bowed, I feel tired suddenly. The Druid has gone. I feel alone. Then I don't. I can sense there is someone else there with me. She is standing in the shadows. Hope I haven't scared her. I thought I was alone. I was.

She hasn't been there that long I feel. Now I can feel the doorway, the portal, between the worlds opening. I feel the urge I have had since I was a child to project my own energy. I get my camera out. Something's going to happen. The air, unusually up here, is incredibly still. I breathe in and exhale slowly. I am walking towards the shadowy woman. I'm going to speak to her but lots of things are happening at once. I am experiencing a feeling that I can most accurately describe as when you are about to orgasm, you know you are and it's too late to stop, no matter what happens. Whoosh. This huge tongue of energy shoots out from my right hand which is holding the staff and flashes between us. Oops. I hear it. I feel it. It crackles and I feel instantly cold. Like it has suddenly taken the heat in my body.

By a wonderful fluke of timing I have managed to photograph it. I can't remember pressing the button but the angels have given me a bit of hand and there it is committed to memory. A perfect blast of energy from one dimension to another. The woman's startled face is captured in the picture. I just can't believe it. The chance of getting that picture are a million to one. Try launching a rocket horizontally and take a picture of it with one frozen hand.

After 700 attempts, give up! Ha! This is just incredible. I'm in shock. I didn't use a tripod, or a long exposure, or any tricks. And I didn't have a bloody big firework up my jumper. And it's not St Elmo's Fire or lightning.

It Came. Out. Of. My. Hand.

This picture should be on every news channel around the world – 'superstitious beliefs real' shock! Take that Rupert Murdoch! If I'd just left it at the description you might have thought 'what a deluded git!'. But I have got a picture of what happened. Angela Davis, the lady in the picture, saw it happen too and you can see the surprise on her face. Pictures. Empirical evidence. How amazing. That should keep Richard Dawkins happy.Or not. And it's a certainty the angels helped with the picture as it is an impossible shot to have got and there is no way I could do that twice. Or even once I suspect. Wow. I need to lie down. This is huge.

The most amazing picture I will ever take. My own energy being projected from my right hand.

10th September 2009

On the way home, still reeling from the significance of what happened last night, I stop by Avebury Stone Circle which I immediately take a dislike to. It feels similar to Stonehenge which to me means my sense is it was created by Dracos or druids in the thrall of this ancient race of controlling monsters. Stonehenge seems to have been constructed with an awareness of the same calendar as the Maya with the Long Count in that it has been calculated that the sun will rise plumb centre of the gap in the stones at the eastern end of the henge on December 21st 2012 when we are back in the universe where we were exactly 26,000 years ago. At the nearest point in the Milky Way to the black hole at its centre.

And the light striking the earth that day will have left the centre of the Milky Way exactly 26,000 years ago. So the light illuminating us on that day will be the light from the stars, or suns, in the centre of the Milky Way which left 26,000 years ago. There is something relentlessly cyclical in this. I walk into the Stones at Avebury which run incomplete round a mile long circle.

I call Angela Watkins and tell her where I am. I instinctively need her focus and energy for a few minutes. Hello darling she trills. I love that woman. If I was dangling from a burning plane with one wing gone I would call her just to hear her say hello darling one last time.

I feel I need to perform a very strange repair on the place. The energy flowing along the ditch dug thousands of years ago around the outside of the stones is flowing in the wrong direction. It is anti-clockwise and that is just not right. I plant my staff in the centre of the ditch and, feeling a little foolish like a modern King Canute trying to push back the tide, I command the energy in the other direction.

My resolve is pathetically weak at first. But then I get pissed off and angry and start to turn into the Incredible Hulk of shamanism! I think I must have read too many Marvel Comics when I was a kid. Someone doesn't like that I am doing this I sense. Tough. It takes all my energy and will to slow the rushing force field and start to run it in the opposite direction. I realize I am talking out loud in that funny ancient language. It's working. I'm sure of it. It is as real as standing in a river and feeling the flow reverse.

Job done, I climb back up to the stones and start walking to the car. A girl is coming towards me. She is carrying a camera. She is a Draco in disguise. She knows I am aware of her. She's uncomfortable as she knows she's been spotted and she is thinking about running. I try my best not to look sinister or threatening. We meet. I say hello and smile. She looks freaked out. When we pass I can hear her steps as she starts to run.

When I turn round she has gone. Disappeared in a flat field half a mile wide. Good trick. When I try to turn my computer on at home later it is dead. I left it in the car at Avebury. It never works again and I have to throw it away. It worked that morning in Glastonbury when I transferred the pictures from the previous night but not now. So there was a great deal of energy flying around at Avebury. I don't think I want to go there again.

Avebury Stone Circle. The ditch where I reversed the flow of the energy running round the ring is behind the stones.

Stonehenge, where the sun will rise between the stones at the east end of the circle on Dec 21st 2012.

Autumn Equinox, Stonehenge. The Equinoxes are the only time the public are allowed into the stone circle.

28th September 2009

Sometimes the angel will visit in numbers. I am listening to Diana Cooper's meditation CD about 2012 and the opportunities for growth it will bring. I'm not convinced about this. My sense is a really unpleasant time will be had by all. We're half way there already as it is. A decade of some of the worst human tragedies I can remember. Oil and food prices are sky rocketing. China and Australia have had their worst droughts in living memory. China is building a $60 billion pipeline to carry water from the south to the northern provinces. Not what you are supposed to think about while trying to raise your vibrational level.

I suppose I am unconsciously feeding the demons of negativity and making my own little contribution to our enslavement. Time to rise above the fear and blackness which resides in my own heart. Didn't used to be like that. What has changed? Why is there this big question mark in my head now? Is my own life which quite frankly is slowly going down the shitter tricking me in to thinking something bad is going to happen? No, no I don't think that's it. There's an urgency, a voice in my head imploring me to listen, to focus, to pay attention. Like I should be to Diana's lovely lilting voice.

She is calling in the angels and a singing bowl is going in the background. And then something brushes my arm. I'm lying on my bed in the dark and that shouldn't have just happened. But there it is again. What feels like calico brushes my arm. And then I have the sense that maybe a dozen angels are silently gathering around me. No, not angels, the disciples. The disciples of Jesus Christ are in my bedroom. I apologise for being negative – that's the sort of thing you do in front of Royalty, you panic and say the lamest things. They calm me and I feel as if I am lifting right off the bed. I am frankly too frightened of what is happening to look.

I remember my Dad saying he felt this happen when my mum was giving him healing for his cancer. He was having chemo at the time and the cancer was spreading but it stopped and disappeared. Maybe it was the chemo, maybe it was Mum. Who knows? Actually, I do. You know when the room is full of people or you are on a bus or train and you shut your eyes and you know they are still there even though you can't see them? That's what this is like. My heart fills with light and happiness and the anxiety recedes.

The disciples are leaving now, their job done. It's as if a light has left the room, not gone out but physically left. Diana does have an extraordinary connection and her presence on the cd caused this visitation. When my wife and I go to listen to her speak in front of maybe 800 people – almost all of whom are female – the orbs are floating around.

Diana Cooper speaking to a live audience. She has just asked everyone to greet their neighbour. Three orbs are visible in a line with a few other faint ones floating around above the happy group.

8th November 2009

Angela Watkins has my wife and I to go along to Barnes Spiritual Church for a session of inspirational speaking and mediumship. I've never seen her in action so this should be interesting. The Church is a beautiful, loving place to be.

But amongst this warmth and love, by contrast I can't help sensing that my wife is reluctant. She is happy enough to come along but it isn't her passion and I can tell that she would rather be somewhere else. But she loves me and wants to show willing. I realize how much I want her to really embrace what is happening to me and take it to her own heart. And then I get this picture of her as a happy little girl playing in the grand Italian Palazzo where she grew up with her brother.

There is something they are playing with from the other side, from the spirit world. Something greedy to have its own soul, which it lacks. That is what poltergeists are. Entities without a soul. They will invade your soul and make you ill or die without conscious volition on their behalf. The most dangerous kind. Their imaginary friend is stealing something from them without them realizing what is happening.

They are too young and too trusting to know any better. It is stealing their childish spirit and covering its tracks by leaving layer upon layer of emotional blockage like a maze. Is that why she is so blocked? Why my angel looks at me blankly when I try to break through to her emotionally? Why she does her crying in secret? Why she is so closed? She will find the missing pieces eventually but maybe not with me. Not in this life.

This possibility makes me suddenly so sad. I have become part of the problem for her, not the solution. The things she loves the most she has learnt to put as far away as possible where they can't be hurt themselves or hurt her. But she won't ever leave me will she? No, that could never, ever happen. I thought my healing energy would eventually heal her wounds. But it's not working is it?

She says she feels she is losing her own identity and dissolving into me. But I feel it was her spirit identity she lost when she was a child. The entity she and her brother used to play with may have stolen it, so I can hardly steal it again.

She says I am overpowering. I don't want to be. I must learn to wind in whatever it is I do. To control and calibrate whatever it is I have. I affect the mood of everyone around me apparently. If I am in a good period everyone loves being around me. I make them laugh and feel good about themselves. I inspire them and encourage them to embrace ideas, theories, a brighter future for themselves.

When I am in my own personal hell, they say they can see black things swirling around me. Shadows flit across the floor and swirl around their hearts, turning them black. I look like a demon when I am angry and it feels as if the sky will burst open. Or something along those lines.

You know when I am around, put it like that.

My wife is starting show signs of relationship fatigue. What were the good things about our relationship are now negatives. Apart from becoming increasingly psychic and wizardly, I am still the same. OK, that's major but I want the same things I used to want. I love her like I used to.

I want her there and to share everything like we always have. But now I am apparently needy. And that's the thing. Women first want you to commit, to need them, then they don't. And need gets a dimunition on the end. A little 'y' turns their desire to change you into the person you could and should be, to rearrange your furniture and your dress sense, into you becoming excess

91

baggage for their journey through life and being needy, ie I don't want you to need me anymore, so get out of my life.

But I am still convinced that would never happen to us. My wife is in it for the long haul. We've never even discussed the possibility of being apart.

Orbs are floating above the people listening to Angela and the other speakers. I've started giving them names now as the same ones show up so consistently. The big bright white one is Uriel. Archangel Gabriel is orange, Chamuel the angel of love is pink. Michael, mighty, mighty Michael, is blue. I take some pictures to capture the moment.

There are so many angels gathered to the right of this picture at Barnes Spiritualist Church they resemble steam.

Archangel Uriel is visible at the top on the right. He is carrying another entity which is the black dot.

Archangel Michael is visible here as the blue orb.

93

This sequence of pictures from Barnes Spiritualist Church illustrates how orbs move around and change from shot to shot. There is a mixture of spirits and angels of protection.

25th September 2009

Fairies at the bottom of the garden are a myth, right? I don't think they are as it happens. I'm staying on the shores of Loch Goil in Scotland at the house of my friend Gary. His son Jack is the one I've mentioned who has a huge orb which appears with him constantly. Gary is an amazing guy with an uncanny knack of seeing an opportunity and driving a truck through it which invariably ends up towing a big trailer full of money as a result. I have helped him work on the house and it is a dream of a place, a fantasy.

Gary has zero interest in what is happening to me and will never discuss it which is fine with me. But whether he likes it or not, he has the best garden fairy collection I have ever seen. The "Boys" come up for weekends of collective midlife crisis management which consists of messing around, walking, bonfires on the beach and fireworks. We're staying this weekend and having a great time. We were here almost exactly a year ago and the manner in which the fairies, elves, esaks and goblins manifest themselves are strikingly similar year on year.

Can hardly believe I just wrote that last sentence. I am an ex-Rugby player who once got stopped by the police (eventually) for riding his motorbike at 150 mph. They didn't fine me for speeding as they couldn't calibrate it as their instruments were off the dial and recorded a blank. (Funny that.) I was using the force to see if I could do it and not kill myself which obviously had worked. They thought I had been drinking when I tried to explain that I was a wizard and therefore invulnerable so I got breathalysed too.

I am not quite this stupid anymore. But it was an interesting experiment nevertheless. But there are fairies at the bottom of Gary's garden. We build a bonfire on the beach and I take some pictures of orbs around my friend Pip Warmouth, one of the greatest landscape painters in the country. He has a go with my camera and takes quite a few himself. Some appear around the bonfire and I capture these angels of love shooting upwards with comet tails. Too fast for embers floating off the bonfire as the length of the tails calculated against the shutter speed indicate they are travelling at around 1,000 mph. The house and the local hotel are populated by a combination of little shooting lights and pudgy orbs.

I have taken several thousand pictures of orbs now and I am becoming pretty good at recognizing different categories. In fact it's like human faces. We are extremely good at recognising and memorizing thousands of faces and it's the same with orbs. They are very consistent. I take some pictures of the outside of the hotel and compare them to the ones I took in the same location a year ago. They are indistinguishable from one another.

On each occasion a group of bright orbs are captured shooting upwards, their tails, created by the speed with which they are travelling, point down. When I walk down to the bottom of the garden next to the boat house, it's as if a group of children on a school trip are following me. I turn round and press the button and the lens is full of them. There is a vast and complex array around us and it ranges from the very high like the archangels and Christ himself to cheeky little pixies and fairies who are forest spirits. They watch over nature and leave the heavy lifting to the archangels, the seraphim and the cherubim.

This is caught up in the dynamics of our universe. A little astro-physics brings the limitless possibilities of the angelic network, the work of the Galactic Elders who watch over us and the God who is the creator and omnipotent power behind everything. And I'm not even religious! I don't accept religious dogma at face value.

Consider this: if you imagine the years which the universe will exist as the atoms which make up everything in that universe, there would not be enough to express it! Not enough atoms to represent the trillions and trillions of years space and time have already passed and what is ahead. Our solar system, which has been around 3.5 billion years already since our sun formed, has about another billion years to go before the sun becomes a red giant and cooks the earth.

Our nearest star, Alpha Centauri, is 4.5 million light years away and will be around for about 14 billion years. It's already a red dwarf so is hard to see amongst the billions of stars around it although they are much further away. The whole history and end of our solar system is less than the blink of an eye in the scheme of things. Yet, we are amazing creatures with dormant powers we are only now relearning to use and rediscovering our link with the beings and consciousness which govern the astonishing dimension in which we live and die.

Anything and everything is possible. When you open your heart, which means allow yourself to feel and believe in the endless possibilities which surround you, you will feel this as a knowing. It's a revelation to give yourself permission to sit in the moment and think what's possible, rather than what isn't. How many times do we have to relearn this lesson in our many lives I wonder?

Two angels moving very fast (possibly 1000 mph) upwards from the fire. Ash is a bit slower to move around.

Pip Warmouth, brilliant landscape painter, and some friends.

This sequence of five pictures were taken near Loch Goil a year apart. What's astonishing is how similar they are!

The orbs are moving upwards very fast. The background is sharp so the blur was not created by camera shake.

A year later. Same hotel, same type of look to the orbs. Very consistent visitors.

And just to make sure for me, this looks like the same orb taken from a different angle a few seconds later.

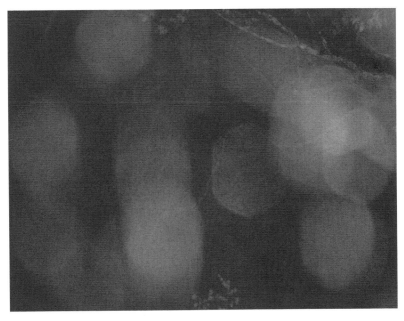

Taken from a series of pictures in the garden at the house in Loch Goil. I felt the orbs were crowding in very close to the lens apart from one where the vanes and patterning are clearer as it is sitting back a bit.

99

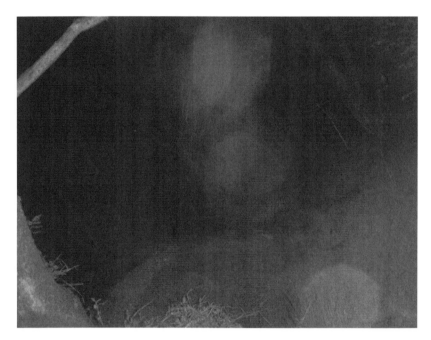

Same garden on Loch Goil with what could be Archangel Chamuel, the love angel, who appears as a pink colour. Gabriel is also thought to appear as red or sometimes orange.

Finally these fairies and angels were taken in my brother's garden at the other end of the country in Kent. Note the same type of angels are present.

1st November 2009

I am remembering who I am. The lock on my third eye has been undone and cast away and I am growing more certain than before about I am exactly. I am a wizard and a sorcerer from previous lives. I have a will, an energy which I can transmit and change things. I feel as if I am not allowed to vent it fully yet as I need to control it fully before I have an accident or destroy something by mistake.

My connection with the Tor is strong and it appears to be my stepping off point for journeys into the cosmos and around our own world. It hums with possibility whenever I am there. It also changes constantly because of its nature as a portal, a gateway to other places. And I am learning from a combination of regressive hypnosis, my own revelations and from channeling by others that I have wielded the ark of the covenant before. You know the thing – it opened up and roasted the Nazis at the end of 'Raiders of the Lost Ark'. It is said to either contain the staff of Aaron or later the Holy Grail, the broken tablets which God wrote the ten commandments for Moses, or the sacred flame of St Germain.

I apparently used it against the walled city of Jericho and it is now hidden in a parallel dimension out of harm's way for the time being and until I can re-learn the necessary skills from previous incarnations. I am a soul rescuer who can help move trapped souls on and I am told I will soon need these skills in a way I can't yet imagine. I have to confess at this point that although I try to stick to my own maxim of open heart, open mind the way you receive information sometimes makes your natural cynicism and lack of trust get in the way.

A lot of this sounds crazy, even to me. But you know what? Again and again, it has a way of coming true or falling into place. And the voice in my head, the voices which float into my head through what I can only describe as my psychic radio receiver, gently urge me to trust in what I am being told and in my own abilities. But it's hard to sometimes. It's just a step too far – even for me. The people around me, the people who love me, humour me as they can see it's so important. But it always comes back to the pictures. The evidence is there permanently in the photographs and yet the questioning and doubt is always swirling round in my head.

What if the sceptics are right? What if I'm chasing rainbows? If I have figuratively forgotten to take the lens cover off? But then. There is so much of it. So many different locations and conditions which have to be more than coincidence. This has been going on for three years now. Will I always doubt myself? How much more evidence do I need? I'm just about to find that out in the most extraordinary week of my life.

18th January 2010

I am at home watching the destruction and chaos in Haiti caused by a direct hit on the capital by a 7.1 Magnitude quake. It looks really bad, couldn't be much worse. Port Au Prince is on a sedimentary flood plain around the river. It's surrounded by granite mountains. Earthquake shock waves slow down in sedimentary rock and bash into each other like the carriages of a train in an accident. It's called amplification and it means everything shakes around more violently.

The unfortunate thing for Port Au prince is the city is full of poorly-built buildings with heavy concrete slabs for floors. The houses built on the granite are untouched. But it's a disaster in a poor country with a dismal history. I'm wishing I could be there now to help.

Later in the day the phone rings. A TV production company want to know if I will go out there and make a documentary. For the first time in my life I get the feeling if I go, I might not come back. I have never had this sense before and it scares me. I am promised armed guards. Good ones. Ex-SAS type good ones. With guns. I want to take Avni, my Kosovan business partner, but it isn't practical. I want someone I can trust to stop me getting killed. It's really in the forefront of my mind.

20th January 2010

We are at Gatwick with a ridiculously huge pile of boxes full of supplies and camera equipment. We have been advised to take our own food, utensils, everything – there's nothing which can be sourced locally. I am nervous and so is everyone else. My cameraman Michael – appropriately named after one of my favourite Archangels – is calm. But then he has just finished filming lions and buffalo in Kenya and I remember how bad-tempered an animal the buffalo is from my own shoots.

The producer and the whole production team are there to see us off. I said goodbye to my wife seriously wondering if I would ever see her again. The problem is no one knows anything about what to expect. The security guys can't pick up their weapons until we get in to Haiti itself and we are looking at a drive through a lawless no man's land between the Dominican Republic and Haiti where stories of muggings, rapes and murders are ringing in our ears.

The production team look even more nervous than I feel. They are thinking the same as me. I am wondering why I agreed to do this. I don't have to. It's only a telly programme. Is it worth the risk? Yes, it is. Am I developing a death wish? Am I secretly hoping I won't make it back?

No, a part of me doesn't care if I make it or not. That is not a nice realization. How can I feel like this? I have discovered angels, I have photographed them. We are not alone. Why then do I want to go? Because I think staying is worse. That is so messed up. On the tarmac waiting our place in the queue to line up and take off for our stop in Sao Paulo, Metatron my guide and keeper of the Stellar Gateway, comes through very powerfully. So strong my head is singing and my heart is thumping. We have work to do in Haiti, he says.

Maybe I will be too busy to get killed. Hope so. Metatron is the angelic evolution of Enoch who helped Michael kick Lucifer out of Heaven. The Christian Church of England took the Book of Enoch out of the Old Testament around 750 AD. It contains huge stories about the work of the angels and I think they must have felt it detracted from the focus on God's work as interest in angels and their power attracted a big increase in attention around this time.

But the Book glorifies God's power. It does provide a lot of detail about the angelic realm and their importance. But it refers to the Nephilim in detail who aren't very popular with the Church – they are referred to elsewhere in the Bible but it was felt they had a hand in the Book of Enoch. The Church felt the Book of Enoch was blasphemous as it depicts fallen angels consorting with mortals and sinning.

The Nephilim were offspring of angels called the Watchers who rebelled and were cast out of heaven. They were incarnated on earth and mated with women (they all seemed to be men - just for a change!). Their distinctive trait was that they were very tall, giants even. The theology about Nephilim is some of their descendants became highly-intelligent and corrupt . It is believed they infiltrate all corrupt concentration of power. It is thought the Nephilim taught mortals astronomy and astrology, the key to nuclear power and how to divide and rule. It's important we are aware of this for our understanding today of the order of Heaven and Earth. Because whatever is not understood about history is doomed to be repeated.

In the Book of Enoch it describes how the Watchers who were the fathers of the Nephilim were cast into a cave and imprisoned for eternity by Archangel Michael and Gabriel. This is what became the Underworld or Hell. Gabriel, feeling compassion for their fate, threw his lyre (a stringed musical instrument) into the pit so that they may console themselves with music. But the lyre was used as a weapon which controlled humans with its beautiful music.

It is also thought that a Nephilim murdered Noah's son Japheth and assumed his likeness. The Nephilim Japheth was responsible for fathering the children who started the tribe which populated Europe after Noah's flood if you can believe such things.

We are in a bizarre hotel in Santa Domingo. When we arrive I walk down the hotel corridor and, judging by the sort of sounds coming from the rooms, it's a certain *kind* of hotel. The tropical fish in the giant tank in reception watch me reproachfully. Reception is a sort of courtyard guarded by a Chihuaha, asleep in a washing up bowl. A man is playing a didgeridoo. We are here to meet an old friend, Roger Bilham, a seismologist from the University of Colorado. Roger and I met in Pakistan and he ended up presenting my programme on the quake by accident.

He is a wild-haired old fashioned British eccentric and one of the world's experts on seismology. He has spent plenty of time making do and sleeping wherever he can in the field. Which is just as well as we have to not only share a room, but a bed, as there has been a mix up. He sleeps cocooned in a sheet like a mummy. I rotate all night like a crocodile with a careless springbok in its jaws.

Michael unpacked the camera kit and found it had been quite seriously damaged in transit and is staying up all night to try and repair it. I have no clue how we are going to get in to Haiti. All flights have stopped as the terminal is leaning at an angle and has been closed. A chopper is going to cost us $30,000 I don't have. I'm out of options right now. We will take care of everything, whispers Metatron in my ear. Sleep, you will need it. I sleep.

21st January 2009

We manage to hire two good 4WD and they leave with our drivers and all our equipment for the border into Haiti. They are like a mobile camping shop. I wonder if I will see either of them again. As promised by my guide Metatron, I have found a way in. The only scheduled flight there is. I cannot believe how many people I am required to bribe. I even get a receipt.

I have put my trust in Metatron to guide me through this and get us all back alive. As the turbo-prop wheels away from us on the grass perimeter at Port Au Prince I wonder if we need to clear customs. That's a joke. No one is in charge and it's everyone for themselves. I told the drivers to find a Union Flag and stay next to it and I would come and find them. We walk past hundreds of makeshift camps of relief workers and armies from around the world. The constant activity and mobilization is right in front of me which was the subject of news reports I saw on the news only a few days ago.

Now I am in the middle of it. I walk the length of the runway with one of my bodyguards. As luck would have it we were dropped at the far end of the runway to where I find my guys, asleep in the 4WDS, right next to the Union Flag as instructed. We return to where we left the others with the gear and we load up. As we drive out through the US Army checkpoint flanked by 50 cal machine guns mounted on army Hummers, I wonder if we will be able to get back in. So I go and find an FBI agent who is checking US passport holders through to be airlifted out. A family of Haitians in their Sunday best are in tears.

They are all cleared to go but the smallest of the children with them is not theirs and doesn't have a US passport. She is the daughter of a distant relative who didn't make it. She isn't allowed through so after some heart searching they decide to stay. I ask the agent how we can best get back into the airport. Should we use the checkpoint? She shrugs, says she doesn't know and that she isn't a travel agent. So much for the special relationship. I get a bit narked and the soldier raises his rifle at me. Doesn't take long does it?

I mentally turn him into a newt and stalk off, fuming. I am walking across some marble tiles which someone has spilt cooking oil on. I skid and fall. My bodyguard tries to catch me but twists me around instead and I crash my knee really hard on the ground. My foot is bleeding. I am wading around in a river of little more than sewage a few minutes later in the centre of town. The destruction and the smell of decomposing bodies is everywhere. We are filming a doco about the geological causes of the quake and its effect but it's impossible to not be deeply affected by what we see. We find ourselves at the Cathedral, a large pink building which features in a lot of the news coverage.

A service was taking place when the earthquake struck and people lie dead under the rubble. I can sense the souls of hundreds of dead wandering around. They are asking me what's happening and what will become of them. I reply and try to reassure them. I feel enormous love and compassion and I know what I need to do. Why I've been led to Haiti and why I accepted the assignment. I take a step back and trip over a body sticking out from the rubble. I fall backwards and land on another one. The skull is crushed in and it is unrecognizable as a person now. I've been filming in the merciless heat of the sun for hours now and I need to rest.

I sit in the front of the 4WD and Metatron is there speaking soothingly in my ear. I should come back and help these souls gathered at the Cathedral to move on. He'll show me how. Back at the airport we find we can drive in easily. In fact no one restricts our movements so we drive around amongst the giant planes parked tightly together on the apron. Do you know how loud a 747 or a C17 army transporter is close up? Very loud indeed. We find our way back to the Union flag and make friends with the British contingent who let us make camp with them. We use their hot water urn to heat our emergency rations which works brilliantly.

They tell us to watch out for the tarantulas. I laugh matily, in on the joke, until one chases me for 50 feet. We spend the night in our tents with the equivalent of Heathrow at its busiest 200 feet away. I sleep for maybe 10 minutes at a time between aircraft movements.

22nd January 2010

Our second day's filming is going well until two policemen sitting in their cruiser are shot dead 200 yards from where we're filming. Dozens of US soldiers pass us on foot accompanied by Humvees and support trucks. The dust trail they kick up is choking as it drifts across us. We could be in Baghdad. That night I ask our security guys if we can return to the cathedral. Roger is up for it.

After some discussion with their boss, they agree it should be OK now we have assessed the threat level. Our bodyguards have both lived in the city for six years so know it well. But even so it's pitch dark, most of the landmarks are now a pile of rubble, and there are people sleeping in the middle of the road so we need to proceed with caution. And they sit directly behind one another in the 4WD.

Apparently this makes it harder for someone to reach in and shoot them both. There is only one moment when they both almost unconsciously slip the safety catch off their weapons as a wild-eyed man sticks his head in the front window to give us directions. After 30 nervous minutes, we drive up to the ruins of the Cathedral in blackness. I can already feel the power rising in me and I am thinking in a language I don't recognise.

This is my grand debut. I jump out of the 4WD followed by the bodyguards. I have both cameras out as I instinctively know I need to record what is about to happen. I am speaking out loud. I know the bodyguard can hear me as they never let me get further than five paces away. They haven't drawn their weapons concealed under their baggy shirts so they can't be unduly worried. Metatron is above the Cathedral. We open the Stellar Gateway.

I am so excited my heart is pounding. I have grounded myself in preparation and I was opening my chakras and concentrating on my crown chakra and third eye as we drove. I am taking pictures and reassuring the frightened souls around the Cathedral. I tell them they are about to fly away to Heaven and everything will be OK. There are thousands of them. And then the angels arrive in their thousands too.

If I was one of these waiting souls I would be able to see a beautiful angelic realm arriving, beckoning and smiling as the angels' wings beat slowly. For an instant, the angels vanish and the tide or current starts to move in the opposite direction as the souls appearing on both cameras start to make their way to Heaven.

And Metatron is working with me to release them as his conduit in the earthly realm. The images which appear on both cameras are astounding. Roger has been watching and listening and is nonplussed. He has seen the little white dots of the angels and the souls appearing and disappearing on my cameras' electronic viewfinders and heard me speaking what sounds like Aramaic or ancient Hebrew. He has been taking pictures too but has seen nothing similar. He wants to know what I am doing and actually what the hell I am. On the way back to the airport I try to explain. In my inexperience I have made several mistakes in finishing the ceremony from which I am yet to suffer the consequences.

There are spirits and Angels of Protection everywhere in Haiti including around our 4WD.

Archangel Uriel appears. There is a group of spirits to the right at the top of this picture. My sense they are a family who were killed together recently in the earthquake.

There were bodies everywhere in Port Au Prince. A lot of people were killed under the rubble of the cathedral where I took this. It is a horrible image but it was a horrible event.

Where the ground had been pulled apart by the movement of the fault line, cracks appeared everywhere.

Seismologist and reluctant tv presenter, Roger Bilham, an Englishman based at the University of Colorado, is an expert on earthquakes. We met on the Pakistan quake and he was my expert on camera for the Haiti film.

The President's palace after the earthquake destroyed it.

My home for a week at Port Au prince airport, Haiti.

Local Haitians were hungry for news and for supplies.

The ground moves up, down and sideways several metres in a big earthquake. This coral reef is now exposed.

Cameraman Michael Hutchinson and I at the Cathedral. It was around this time I started to realize what my real mission was and what I had to do that night. I could feel confused and frightened souls around me.

Streets and streets of flattened buildings full of corpses. The smell of decomposition was everywhere.

113

At first there was nothing visible at the Cathedral but I could feel the Stellar Gateway opening for the trapped souls.

And then it happened in an instant. Legions of Angels came to greet the dead.

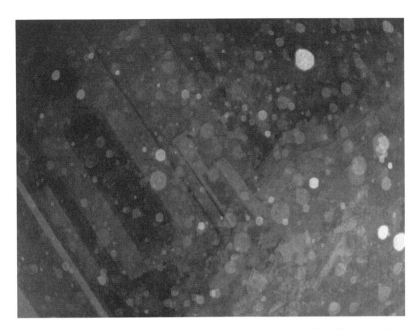

I couldn't believe my eyes as I greeted the Angels in something like Aramaic.

And then it was as if the tide turned and I could feel the energy flowing into the Stellar Gateway. This was about 8 seconds after the previous picture.

115

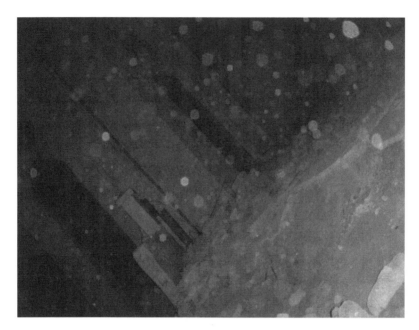

Souls were dancing past me on their way to Heaven through the Stellar Gateway in increasing numbers. There are Angels in this picture too. The Angels are hexagonal and they are radiating energy. The souls are more amorphous.

Archangel Uriel is arriving. He is the bright orb on the right. His remit is to protect us from earthquakes and floods.

As the souls disappear and the moment passes, Uriel is still there.

Two lovely cynics, seismologist Roger Bilham and cameraman Michael Hutchinson check their own cameras – just in case!

117

The image of the souls is fading on camera 2 which I was using simultaneously as they depart.

24th January 2010

We fly back to Santo Domingo. Eventually. The first plane won't start so they find another which arrives with only one engine running. This is to avoid two start up costs to the airport. So not all commerce has died on its feet then. We cram our gear in and climb aboard, grateful to have made it. There is only one flight out a week and this is it. Our clothes never arrived on the flight in – someone was obviously making some choices on what went and what didn't on the overloaded plane and I have lived in the same shorts and shirt for a week.

I am filthy and I smell really bad. I think about another flight we took out of Simelue, an island off Indonesia, when I was in a similar condition after the tsunami in 2004. The little transport plane was so full I was sitting on the floor between the seats. Wouldn't get that at Heathrow. There was so much water on the runway from the tropical downpour we only just got up to take off speed in time and made it over the wire perimeter fence with half a metre to spare.

My daughter Betty sneaked her precious "Mousey" which she's had since she was born into my rucksack for good luck so I thought I'd make a pictorial record of Mousey's Holiday in Haiti. It was a little bizarre but it cheered me up and made Betty laugh.

Mousey demonstrates the standard of accommodation on his holiday and the proximity to the runway. No sleep for anyone.

119

An accomplished pilot, Mousey runs through the pre-flight checks in the helicopter before our tour of Haiti from the air.

Even energetic, world class scientists get tired. None of us had really slept for four days and we were exhausted.

25th January 2010

Back in the Dominican Republic we are rewarded for our work to release the souls at the Cathedral. After two days camping at the airport, the rather splendidly-named Airbridge Controller who hails from Jakarta, Indonesia takes pity on us. He barters Roger agreeing to be earthquake expert and greet a UN politician on behalf of Haiti to debrief her on the quake, which he does brilliantly, in return for the promise of a ride back over Haiti.

This is so we can film from the air, an essential angle for the film. I am calm. I know we will be OK. We have one of the most powerful beings in the Universe helping guide us. I can't believe I just wrote that sentence. But it makes sense to me. Maybe I am crazy. Exhausted certainly.

We're hanging round the little control building watching life pass us by. We take pictures of one another. And then suddenly a huge passenger helicopter becomes available. ERA, the wonderful, kind, US company who own the heli, need to drop medical supplies around the country at various hospitals. Which means they are about to do a quick circuit of the whole country.

We are shoved on board and are already taxying as I call the office back in the UK to tell them what is happening and to get us insured. Roger is receiving coordinates for the fault line and NASA pictures of the area so we will recognise it when we see it. It couldn't run smoother. We stop off and deliver supplies and film the fault line from the air.

But it's not where it should be and we realize we are looking at a different fault line to the one we expected to find. There are TWO! This is a big deal for Roger as a seismologist, giving him a world exclusive, and us in to the bargain for the film. Whole sections of the coastline have sunk into the sea and other sections have been pushed up by the movement of the fault. Coral reefs are now exposed to the air and trees along the shore are submerged almost to their tops.

We land back in Santo Domingo feeling triumphant. I say a silent prayer of thanks to Archangel Metatron for watching over us. We are so relieved and excited by what we've discovered we laugh all the way back to the hotel in the tiny taxi with our benevolent Rottweiler bodyguards hitting their heads on the roof in the third row of seats at the back.

The closest we come to death is now as we drive back into town through some of the scariest, suicidal traffic I have ever encountered. But we are very relieved we are still alive and going home. I am beginning to feel rather strange and extremely tired. I take this to be stress and exhaustion, which, partly, it is. But it is something else.

Michael Hutchinson and I are back in London - just. Santa Domingo airport had a total power cut just before our flight was called and we had to find our way to the gate, using my headtorch, my sixth sense and a guiding mobile phone being waved at the gate by ground staff. There was no other indication of where the gate was. The British pilot took off with just the flare path working and nothing else. Roger Bilham is heading home to Colorado. We hand the footage we have shot to the waiting production assistant at the airport. There is a week before the programme is broadcast so there's no time to lose. She looks at our grey, strained faces and asks if we are OK.

I don't feel OK. I want to cry. We both have food poisoning and are as weak as kittens. The camera gear went AWOL when we changed flights in Spain, so we missed our connecting flights and took it in turns to try and find the missing gear in between running to the toilet. Very wizardly - not. I have had food poisoning before but this is much worse. I can hardly stay conscious in the cab home.

I sleep for almost two days and I feel a bit better. This is nowhere near post traumatic stress disorder but it's pretty bad. I find my wife in a restaurant with an old friend. They ask me how it went and I start to cry for all sorts of reasons, all at once. It's a mixture of relief, exhaustion, horror, sadness and delayed shock about what I witnessed at the Cathedral. These events are Biblical in the way they happen. I looked up a passage in Revelations about an earthquake which left bodies piled in the street and it was a perfect description of Haiti. I am coming back to Revelations too often. Too often.

I am still connected to the Cathedral. I can feel the silver cord is attached to the energy required to move those souls on. It is attached to me and it is draining me. I was so excited when it happened I forgot to hand the silver cord off, close down my chakras and ground myself. Basic stuff but I left Haiti wide open, shining like a star.

4th February 2010

I need to offload the cord on the Tor. Don't ask me why. I just do. I make the long drive down, half dead. The climb to the Tor is ten times as long as usual but the familiar little tower on top of the hill feels welcoming and positive. They are waiting for me. The Maya guide and my North American Indian guide are waiting for me. I carefully call in the ancestors using my singing bowl. My staff is alive in my hands. The Maya guide, Quetzalacoatl, comes into me and I become him. I am wearing a beautiful headdress of turquoise feathers.

My face is painted white like a bald eagle. My staff is a ceremonial axe with feathers hanging from it. I circle and soar like an eagle around the Tor, chanting and uttering spells in the tongue of the Maya. My Indian guide sweeps around us approvingly in the form of another eagle. I lift the cord from my shoulders and offer it to the Stellar Gateway. It is accepted and snakes away into the heavens. Immediately this happens, I start to feel better. I wheel on the air currents with my Guides and gulp in the freezing air with grateful gasps. Next time Mr Would Be A Wizard, remember the basic steps Angela taught you.

On Glastonbury Tor, freezing cold, channeling my Maya guide. I am releasing the silver cord from Haiti. I look ridiculous. Like a chicken. Sometimes reality is separated by a very long way from the vision in your head.

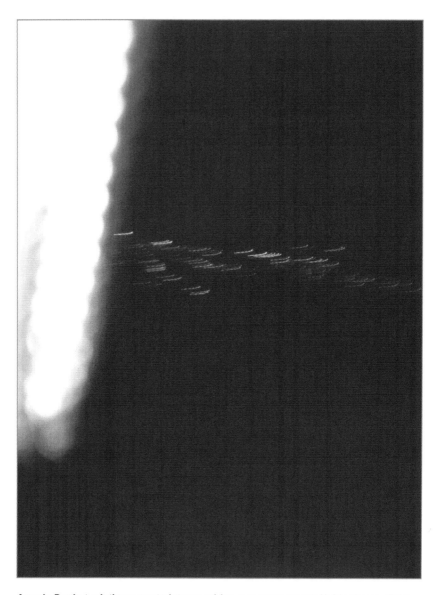

Angela Davis took these next pictures with my camera on my Haiti release night on Glastonbury Tor. They are very strange. I have no idea what this is but it shouldn't be there. She was moving the camera while the shutter was open judging by how much the street lights in the background are blurred but the light in the foreground looks like it is moving with her as it isn't blurred. The street lights are further away and would therefore show more movement as she moved the camera.

And again but note how there is an absence of light behind the streak. That shouldn't look black.

Then Angela took a series of pictures where a totally black shadow crept across the lens incrementally. Could this be Archangel Metatron's dark energy?

Again, there is no reason for this shadow. I can feel its energy pressing on the right hand side of my face as I write this caption. Very strange.

And then it was gone. This is what the half-dark shots should have looked like.

6th February 2010

The voices of the angels are growing stronger in my ear. Whenever I am still, I can feel their presence. Walking through Richmond Park with the dogs, up on the roof of the house on the decking at night, when I am driving, swimming, lying in bed at night, they are there. Sometimes I imagine them hovering in mid-air, their wings flapping slowly, or just standing next to me peacefully, wings folded. They want as many people as possible to feel their presence and hear their words.

They want me to tell others about what I am experiencing so they will know too. It's simple. I've heard them, seen what we are convinced are actual images of them and other intelligent beings which exist around us. They say they are more present when they are needed - like now. The human race has lost its centre, its soul, and as a consequence we are rudderless.

To fill this emptiness, we resort to other things like alcohol, drugs and instant gratification. There is an unquenchable thirst we cannot slake and a hunger we can't satisfy. There is a fear we are alone, that this is all there is. But it isn't. There is so much more if you stop and listen to your inner voice for a while and maybe pay attention to the angels and archangels around you. They are there.

If I say the Nephilim walk the earth, apart from what I've already explained about them, you may not know any more than that. It's interesting they haven't had more of an impact on our consciousness and I'm not clear why their apparent existence is not talked about more. People talk of a conspiracy by the media to keep their existence a secret but it is beyond me why that should be. The Nephilim were thought to be a race of angels who came to earth in humanoid form after angels mated with humans. What distinguished them from everybody else was they were sometimes very tall, had wings hidden under their clothes, had blue eyes, sweeping cheekbones and blue blood. Sounds outlandish?

Goliath was supposed to be one – remember he was the Philistine who was defeated by a little Israelite guy called David who killed him with a slingshot and went on to lead the Israelites against the Egyptians, the Pharisee and the Hittites? The Nephilim took earthly women as their wives and the descendants of their children are thought to still be around today which might explain the enormous average height of some African tribes and modern day giants. Now here's the really strange bit.

If you Google Nephilim images, you will come up with dozens of pictures of perfect giant skeletons up to fifty high which have been unearthed on archaeological digs all over the world, particularly Turkey. But why isn't it talked about more? I just don't know. Perhaps influential leaders are rubbing them out of the picture still? The Book of Enoch was removed from the Bible for being blasphemous. It mentioned the Nephilim and giants. But then there is a discussion to be had here about how controversial information is handled by the media and governments. The Book of Enoch has been suppressed for hundreds of years by the Church and that is probably where the stigma comes from.

The contents of my diary probably won't make it on to the front pages although it should. 'Angels Exist', 'Reincarnation Confirmed', 'There Is A God' or 'World To Reinvent Itself' are never going to splashed across the front page of the tabloids but it would be wonderful if they were because to my mind their significance and relevance to every one of us far outweighs who's been caught with their pants down, or wearing someone else's pants or not wearing any pants at all.

My Mum used to cause some raised eyebrows when she talked in a matter of fact way about the existence of angels and was written off as a harmless nutter. Now I have hundreds, thousands of photographs of things which defy any rational explanation. Actual photographs, taken on different cameras, all over the world, in hugely varying conditions, and by lots of other people I've met too.

And the funny thing is the skeptics, who dismiss it as easily-explained flotsam and jetsam floating about in the air, can never offer up the hundreds of pictures they have taken themselves which demonstrates their point. And the reason is they can't because they don't have any. But they will try to provide a rational explanation based on dust, cheese, fibres, indigestion, anything rather than embrace what is staring them in the face. And usually they dedicate 0.1 seconds thought and zero research to the subject before dismissing it out of hand. It's just not important to them. And that is the power of programming, control, manipulation, call it what you will.

25th February 2010

I am going to try my ability as an exorcist out today. I'm not planning anything big or expecting Linda Blair to start rotating her head and spraying green stuff down me. My good friend Pauline lives in a house in Kent which she says is full of odd things. There is the black entity in the bedroom which looms over her at night and fills her with dread. It stops her sleeping. When I go in her bathroom which is a lovely bathroom as they go, I can hear whispering and I feel as if something doesn't want me there.

Pauline is a fascinating person. Without it being a biggie, when she and I first met at Angela Watkins's mediumship class we immediately sensed we were married in a previous life and lived as woodcutters in the forest. It feels like it was in the middle ages. We lived in a wattle and daub cottage with a thatched roof with mud from the farm animals and the rain splashed halfway up the white walls. We collected wood which was turned into charcoal in burners.

The wood was piled up and covered in rolls of turf. It was burnt slowly until it turned to charcoal. There was always a pot of something bubbling away in the cottage and wood smoke from the fire heating the pot curled up and out into the sunlight twinkling through the canopy of trees above. It was when almost all of England was covered by forest. We had a happy life together and lived to be old. Maybe it explains why we are calm together.

There is no "unfinished business" as it were. Pauline is very sensitive and struggles to keep visiting spirits and all sorts at bay. It seems any house she lives in becomes active simply because she is there. This particular place is an old building and I sense it had a few residents who were there before her. I connect with the entity in the bedroom who lacks a soul so it is hard to know how to get rid of it. You can't engage with something which lacks life or intelligence. Although I can sense it I don't have a clue how to get it to leave.

So I just use my will to push it from the room and out through the window, blocking its way back in mentally. I visualize a fence of protective energy around the walls of the bedroom and bless its sanctity. I announce that this room is now sacred and must not be interfered with. I rap my staff on the shagpile three times for good measure and the familiar low boom and a dark blue wave like on a very large glass of flaming Sambuca rolls out in my mind from the centre of the room. That should do it. The voices in the bathroom belong to two grumpy old women in Victorian scullery maid's outfits.

I let my Mongolian yaks teeth necklace spin to feel the energy and where it is concentrated. I can feel it through my feet too. I am re-grounding myself constantly to protect my own aura from harm. Once I've identified where I feel the presence of the old ladies is strongest I use the bone on the necklace to extract the energy which is planted in the bathroom. I make a sort of 'sssssssiiiipppp...shhhhhh' sound as I suck the dark energy wrapped round the bathroom out and expel it.

I learnt this technique for extracting unwanted energies off a shaman from Bhutan. It's the first time I've tried this as a sort of doctor's visit but I feel it has gone quite well. As I'm leaving Pauline waves from the doorway. I can sense the two old ladies behind her, also waving. Maybe I need a little more practice.

20th May 2010

The Chilean earthquake followed Haiti by a month. I have been asked to fly out to Chile and work with another geologist, Mike Beavis, who is an expert on the Chilean fault line. Chile holds a world record for the most violent shock ever recorded in 1960: 9.5 on the Richter scale.

On this trip I sense very strongly that Sandalphon, Metatron's twin, is riding with me and there is more soul clearing to do. This is one of those experiences where I feel I am being given a message. There is a song by Sara Maclachan called suitably, 'Angel'. I think it is probably the most beautiful song I have ever heard. It's never been a particular hit internationally as a single but a lot of people seem to know it.

It's playing on the radio in the cab on the way from home to Heathrow. When we pick up the hire cars at Santiago airport in Chile I switch on the radio and 'Angel' is playing. In Chile. We drive to Valparaiso on the coast and when I walk into the hotel the same song is playing. The angels are saying they're there to greet me clearly. It' so odd I record it playing in the hotel just to make sure I'm not hallucinating.

Chile contrasts very strongly with Haiti. The earthquake damage is relatively light as the buildings in the main were built to be earth-quake proof. Considering it was an 8.8 magnitude quake as opposed to Haiti's 7.1, it's astonishing how little building damage there is. The worst effect seems to have been the tsunami which inundated the coastline around Concepcion in the south where the centre of the shock was based. We visit a suburb of Concepcion for dinner and I'm drawn to the streets around the restaurant.

Tsunami damage in Chile. We estimated the wave at 30 feet high.

I take some pictures and there are crowds of orbs in some but I am struck by a formation of four blue orbs which appear as if they are moving in a coherent shape together past someone's front door. South America has seen its fair share of murder and war. The Spanish Conquistadors, the French, English, Dutch and so on have travelled down the continent murdering and being murdered in turn. I can sense souls going back hundreds of years who are still around. I instinctively perform a shamanic ceremony of release every night in my hotel room which leaves me exhausted. My wife rings me late one night. I can't even remember which continent she is on. I can hardly remember where I am myself I am so tired and jetlagged. She is in China.

I fall asleep talking to her and I wake up half an hour later to find she is yelling down the phone at me to close the line as it is costing her a dollar a minute. Still feel stupid about doing that. Chile is a very long country. We drive 600 miles and there is still more ground to cover. Katie Brimblecombe is on her first overseas shoot as production manager and she is doing a brilliant job. Katie is a very sensitive soul and can feel what I feel. She is becoming a sorceror's apprentice before my eyes. Lovely.

We fly down the southern coastline in a helicopter and are amazed by the spectacular, wild Southern Ocean scenery. Because the upheaval caused by the quake was so enormous, it has made the entire continent rise three metres. A green band of rock is clearly visible above the waves and the shoreline where it has risen up out of the water. Beaches which were 25 metres wide are now 100 metres in width as the beach has risen out of the water. The quake displaced such a large mass of rock it has slowed the earth's rotation a tiny but measurable amount.

Cameraman Chris Sutcliffe and geologist Mike Bevis practice not falling over in an earthquake in Chile.

This shot I took from the helicopter over an outlying island near the earthquake epicenter shows how the coastline has changed. The water permanently no longer reaches the harbour.

Cameraman Chris Sutcliffe and geologist Mike Bevis next to a section of rock which has been pushed up over 2 metres by the Chile 8.8 earthquake. This uplift has taken place around the whole of the southern half of South America. Archangel Sandalphon was with me the entire time as I connected with this country and continent.

Archangels can cross the Milky Way in the blink of an eye. Humans take a little longer but a helicopter is still a quick way of getting around nevertheless when there are no roads.

The coastline of the South Ocean around the bottom half of Chile is wild and beautiful and I thought about the thousands of years of conflict, ingenuity and mystical genius this land has seen. It's like being on another planet.

This building in Concepcion, Chile became famous as a landmark after the earthquake. At night I found it was surrounded by orbs.

There were orbs everywhere in Chile and I got the sense that there were many ancient spirits close by.

If I stayed in one area and radiated, more and more orbs would congregate. I loved the ancient energy. This is the continent of the Maya, the Incas and the Aztecs.

These three pictures were taken over a few minutes in the same street. I had the feeling they were passing right through me.

Everywhere I went in Chile I was surrounded by activity.

This was incredible! A neat formation of four Archangels flying along together. They moved across to the left and continued down the street!

I swung the camera round to the left to follow them as they were visible to the naked eye and you can see the same orbs from the previous picture moving away down the street!

This was right next to the building which broke in half in Concepcion pictured earlier and there is a beautiful orb in the top right of the shot. I can't be sure, but I think it might have been Hades, Greek God of the Underworld and the brother of Zeus. I'm not sure, because Hades is not one of my guides. I only feel certain about Deities who are a little closer to home for me.

138

This next sequence feels to me like Hades (top right) is moving round to draw out trapped souls and take them to the Underworld. Not ideal as far as I am concerned.

I think that large grey orb to the right is still Hades. A lot of souls are coming to him from the wrecked building. It doesn't mean necessarily that's where they lived before they died but it's where they have congregated. I was drawn to this area and I felt it was a portal like Glastonbury Tor.

139

If it is Hades, he is now sitting right in the centre of this shot a few seconds later.

The final shot shows a neat, well organized grouping following Hades who is bottom right.

27th May 2009

Back in Glastonbury again I meet the first person I have encountered who genuinely does not seem to be human. I talk to him for two hours and he answers my questions about our ancestors, the Dracos, the Galactic Elders, aliens, other beings, unicorns…anything and everything I can think of to throw at him. And he speaks fluidly and unhesitatingly. He's a strange-looking fish anyway. Very tall and bony. But there is nothing I can engage with him on which is earthly like his favourite food, places he has visited, his childhood. After two hours I realize we have spoken about every manner of crazy thing, just nothing whatever about him personally.

My skill is getting a bead on someone's makeup, the definition of their essence as people. Happy, sad, positive, negative. With this guy, nothing. He thinks he has been chosen as a mouthpiece for an ancient race of aliens who walk amongst us on earth called the Greys – the classic little men they found in the crashed UFO at Roswell.

He describes their scouts as tall, pale, hairless beings who like to disguise their identities by wearing long coats, hats and sunglasses. He says they can levitate so they float above the ground. I remember a friend's mother sitting me down once and describing exactly these sort of figures. She claimed they had been floating in the air above her car as she drove home along a country lane one night. She was adamant about what she had seen and very specific. I believed her. After I leave I feel very disconcerted about the meeting. My sense is I have just been talking to my first alien.

9th June 2010

I am going to tell you an odd little tale now about a murder which has happened almost right outside our house. And it illustrates that the angels will never quite leave me alone and that there is always work to do.

I look out of the window and there is a body lying on the pavement, covered in a brown sheet. Police are everywhere. I stare at the body. I know who it is. I know. The police come round to take copies of our security camera footage as they cover the pavements immediately around the house and might yield some evidence. Security cameras are great for capturing orbs at night by the way. They go into infra red mode which is perfect for seeing the occasional orb. They float into view, dance around to show off and say hi I'm here, then whizz away at speed at odd angles. I ask the policeman if the murder victim's name is what I think it is.

He denies it but it's easy for me to know. It is him. What's strange is the murdered man has some history with us. I once caught him torturing his pregnant dog by repeatedly kicking a ball at her. The dog was whimpering in pain and fright and I asked him to stop. He almost took my head off so I went home and called the RSPCA as what he was doing to the dog was cruel. It turned out they knew this character well and he had a history of animal abuse. The dog was taken off him and he was banned from ever owning another one.

To express his gratitude he slashed the tyres of the vans we owned at the time for our dog walking business which we used to park outside the house. Each van had to be put on the back of a breakdown truck and taken to Kwik-Fit for four new tyres each. £3,750 later we were back in business although there were a lot of dogs crossing their legs. Oh and he threw in threatening to kill my wife when he bumped into her in the street and boasted about what he'd done. So there wasn't much love lost between us. I am walking past the spot where he died that night and I can feel him standing there. He is asking where he is and why no one can see him. He says he is very scared as he doesn't understand what has happened to him.

I ask him if he would like some help to go on his way. He nods and says he's sorry for everything which happened between us and for everything else he's done. I ask him if he knows what the Akashic record is and he says they are waiting to show him his life and he doesn't want to go. I tell him he must and it will be OK. He will go to Heaven once he's seen the error of his ways. With a quick glance both ways up and down the street, I recite a prayer of release in my funny language and take pictures. Metatron is there and the Stellar Gateway opens to receive him. Reluctantly he lopes off and doesn't look back once. The orb floating above the pavement gradually fades until it is no longer visible.

The spirit of a murdered man over the spot where he died.

After I perform the ceremony, the dead man's spirit is gone.

13th June 2010

Today is my birthday. Tomorrow is our 13th wedding anniversary and we are still going to go out and celebrate at the restaurant we went to the day we got married. 13 has always been my lucky number.

19th June 2010

Pauline has dragged me off to Somerset to attend a Retreat. This is where students work with spiritual advisors to help in their development and rid themselves of negative energy or anything else holding them back.

We go out into the woods and I manage to lose the others. I find them again and everyone has chosen a tree to commune with. This is normally good fun and I have grown to love a good hug with a tree. I love trees and they are very grounding. Those roots are a great visualisation of grounding. The most important practice you will ever learn. Terry, our leader, finds me and I suddenly feel mortally afraid. Not because of him. He seems harmless. Afraid of myself or what I was holding in.

He is also the best exorcist in the country so I am keen to watch and learn. He approaches me and says really quietly, so only I can hear, 'you can't do anything until you let this go' and he taps my heart chakra. Wow. The tears really come on and I literally fall to the ground amongst these beautiful, ancient trees and sob my heart out. Really sob. Big, wracking girly sobs. My strength is gone.

I have tears smeared down my face mixed in with leaves and bits of twig. Snot bubbles out of my nose. This has to be as bad as its going to get. I feel like the sadness I have accumulated in my life is choosing this moment to erupt. Oh strewth I can't bear this. I am not strong enough. Uriel, Michael and Gabriel are suddenly around me. I can feel their compassion and strength.

It's the first time for what seems like a long time I have experienced this. I think I have been projecting so much chaotic energy it has disrupted the vibrational frequency around me. I sit up and pay attention to my environment. I stop crying. The Archangels float above me. They are so beautiful you know? You really have to get yourself plugged into this again. It's brilliant. Of course it helps if you are a bi-polar emotional cripple. It really gives it an extra edge.

What I was looking at while I sobbed my heart out.

145

20th June 2010

Day two of the retreat and I am already dreading what's coming. At the end of the day, we are going to have a healing session with Terry. Healing? That's a laugh. This guy is one of the most powerful people spiritually I have ever met. No wonder he can ghost bust. This isn't going to be a healing session for me, it's going to be an exorcism. He knows it. I know it.

And the prospect of what might happen is stressing me out. The day starts gently with a little meditation and spiritual aerobics on the lawn. While I'm trying my best not to fall asleep a chicken and a cat come and sit on me. That happens a lot. A regular Mary Poppins, me. Right - time for the healing.

This is fascinating actually. For some reason war has broken out between Natalia, the other person who leads these courses, and Pauline. I get the sense Natalia has taken exception to one of Pauline's previous incarnations – a tragic witch with a dislike of children. Ironic that Pauline is the loveliest person you could hope to meet and is a …teacher. See how that works Karmically?

Terry lets me work with him on a lady who we can feel was hanged in a previous life. She starts to choke and I can sense the rough hessian of the rope around her neck. It's quite scary in a way observing a sweet, elegant woman reliving her death throes with all the anger and sadness. Terry is uncoiling long strands of black energy which is stuck in her body and dragging it out. He cuts it off at the base, ties it in a metaphorical knot and disposes of it over his shoulder. Funny, that's what I do. Then it's my turn.

As soon as he puts his hands on me as subject I can feel the resistance. With some coaxing and not so gentle coaxing, all manner of emotions, memories, past lives and lurking energies are extracted. I'm aware but completely incapable of autonomous movement. I think if he'd stabbed me at that moment there would have been nothing I could or wanted to do about it. It's actually an incredible experience.

He does it with the Scissor Sisters, Joss Stone and the Doors playing quite loudly. The energy and emotion of the music seems to help him and it doesn't seem incongruous. When Terry has finished with me I snap back into my body as if nothing had happened. Altogether satisfying. While I was out of my body I saw Merlin, King Arthur, Metatron and an army of Dracos represented by Egyptian gods like Anubis and Set who are depicted as jackal gods, ie men with the heads of jackals. This was what appeared in my dream last year and inserted the implant in my head.

Oh my God I sound like a classic paranoid schizophrenic. Ooh yes, they are after me doctor. I am pursued by half men half jackals who sometimes appear as that monster out of Alien. But if I'm honest, really honest, the vision I just experienced seemed real. I had the dream. And that's the point, you do just know. But hey, that's my reality. What's yours?

21st June 2010

Last day of the Retreat and we are on the cliffs overlooking the sea. It's a beautiful day. We are in a circle, meditating and working on our chakras. I am pretty open. In my mind's eye aka my third eye in my forehead, a door opens in mid-air and this troop of about 50 little Samurai appear and encircle the ring we have formed. I am freaked out.

They are black. Their Samurai helmets, armour and swords are perfect miniatures. They are about three feet tall. I am talking to them. Well to thin air actually. A few concerned eyes which had been closed open and peer at me. Clearly lost what little of his mind was left. But I feel their presence. They are my little soldiers. They are the things Angela tried to explain a year earlier. Little black Darth Vaders. I really do have a lot of protection and if I think about it I would look into the pit and meet Abaddon's furious glare.

Maybe the Devil is the ultimate client for the angelic realm. If it could be saved, could that save the world?

Looking for the little Samurai men. This is where they appeared to me in my mind's eye.

147

22nd June 2010

Next day at Mary Magdalene's church in Taunton, I catch a huge orb in the vestry on camera. I feel it is an angel of protection. The Magdalene ley line which is thought to pass right through the Abbey in Glastonbury runs down the nave of the church. I stand at the altar with my dowsing crystal. After a few seconds I realise it is hitting my arm because it is spinning so violently that it is horizontal. That is definitely one powerful ley line.

Archangel Metatron in as clear a shot as I'm ever going to get. Archangel Uriel is also thereby the altar although he is further away so appears smaller.

Here they are again. Metatron and Uriel.

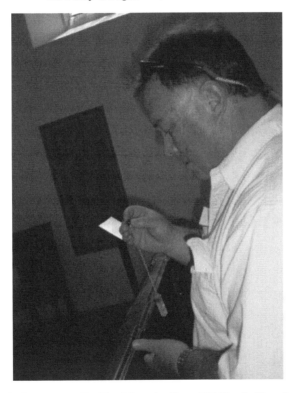

I am standing in the nave on the Magdalene ley line of St Mary's Church, Taunton. My dowsing crystal went nuts.

18th July 2010

My wife is in Shanghai and she has paid for me to fly out and join her. Upper Class on Virgin. My friend Angela Davis is convinced I am going to die while I'm there which is frightening me.

I feel suicidal. It's not the first time in my life. I have always been afflicted with sudden bouts of depression after a prolonged high when I feel indestructible and full of ideas. It isn't triggered by anything tangible. It just happens with no warning like a balloon suddenly deflating. I can't help feeling that my life is over.

I find my wife running a fascinating event at Shanghai Expo She is so clever, my wife. I see her for the first time after I arrive in Shanghai as she stands quietly to one side at the front of the room. She is wearing some earrings I bought her and is dressed in black as usual from head to foot. She looks so sweet and sexy I want to run up and hug her.

We have a lovely time the next day sightseeing. I am amazed by Shanghai. What a vibrant, optimistic place. Everyone has a job and is busy going somewhere. We ride on the Maglev train out to the airport just for fun. It is such an engineering marvel it is like kissing God. 410 kph with no oscillation whatsoever. You could sit with a saucer of tea balanced on your head and it wouldn't spill. We hold hands.

I start crying at the pureness of the train's smooth ride and the pureness of the love I feel for my wife. This is how I feel about God and the angelic realm. I love them for their purity and shining, white, brilliant love. Nice train I say and squeeze her hand. She smiles at the 5 year old sitting next to her. (Me.) Am I ever going to grow up? Maybe not. Maybe I don't want to. I love the child in my heart. It's keeping me alive.

We go for drinks in the Financial District and sit admiring the magnificent view across the river. As dusk comes, the buildings light up. Literally. It's like an architectural firework display. We talk for hours. I can't remember anything we discuss. All I can remember is thinking my wife is the most amazing person I have ever met. Who wouldn't?

To every person suffering the same circumstances or feeling very low for whatever personal sadness or tragedy you are facing I am sending you the biggest hug ever and a blessing from every Angel there is. You are loved, you know? We all are. There is a ball of Archangel Rafael's green healing energy available for each and every one of you. I wish you all the love there is in the Universe.

I am rubbing my hands together right now and forming the ball of energy in my hands and now I'm blowing it to you gently with my love. Can you feel it? You should be able to. Healing others makes me feel good and lifts my spirits.

The Thomas Hetherwick-designed 'Hedgehog' was the UK Pavilion at Shanghai Expo. I thought it was the best. Each rod contained some seeds.

I feel like committing suicide – very, very long story. Doesn't look like it does it? My wife is my rock and I love her.

Still, it is a great view of Shanghai, even if my life feels like it's over temporarily.

22nd July 2010

On the way to the airport. I am in the back of a big, black limo owned by the hotel. The six lane highway is almost empty. 'All We Ever Do Is Say Goodbye' by John Mayer is playing.

Perfect.

I am crying.

The chauffeur is trying admirably hard not to but is glancing at me in the rearview mirror. He's probably thinking I am sad to be leaving such an incredible city and in a way he is right.

On the flight I spend hours being consoled by the sweetest man I have ever met. He's one of the cabin crew. He's a gay man from Italy and to be honest the kindness he shows me is almost enough to win me round. I sit at the bar in Upper Class and he feeds me good espresso coffee, whisky, biscotti and a delicious prawn curry he conjures up. Bless you lovely gay man, wherever you are. You singlehandedly restored my faith that night. I'm sorry I cried over your waistcoat. I am such a big baby. But angels appear just when you need them in all guises, they really do.

4th September 2010

I have met two of the most extraordinary individuals. It started over lunch with someone I had never met before. We get to talking and I know he is one of us immediately. His head sort of radiates energy which cracks and sparks off him. I feel immediately that he is somehow connected to the Divine Feminine like me. I think of the Shekinah as I speak to him. I ask him if there is anybody he is close to who is associated in some way with the Divine Feminine. He looks startled, defensive, then curious. A little tic develops under one eye.

He is in a relationship with a woman who he thinks is somehow very special. He tells me she is the incarnation of Persephone who, in Greek Mythology, was the consort of Hades. I can sense Hades' presence. I'm not sure if I quite trust this entity. He was Zeus's brother for starters and is the Gatekeeper to the Underworld. In Egyptian history, Osiris the High Priest, performed the same role. Osiris is depicted as a priest with a rod clasped in his right hand, held across his chest. In Christianity, or the Book Of Enoch to be exact, Metatron – my guide – is the gatekeeper of the Stellar Gateway which I have started to work with so much. So that makes Hades my nemesis in theory. There is a tickle of resistance from my new friend. I have to meet Persephone though.

Persephone cooks the most fabulous roast chicken dinner with all the trimmings. I can't stop looking at her – it's almost pathological. I feel I am in the presence of something quite extraordinary. For a start, there is something very unusual about her pupils. I'm not quite sure if she is wearing contacts. Her eyes are flecked green like a cat. In fact her cat which is snowy white has one green and one red eye itself.

For some reason I think of Odysseus and the Sirens who draw him and his ship onto rocks and they are lost. Odd image to come to mind. She shows me her ring which is made from pink garnet or cornelian. It is cracked in the centre and engraved with a sort of intaglio script which looks like it could be Aramaic. She tells me how she woke up in hospital after a failed suicide attempt when she was 16 and the ring had appeared on her finger. She hasn't taken it off since, ever.

My sense it was a wedding ring from Hades. She says she became conscious of his presence after the ring appeared. I also get the sense that she has the chance in this life to do something amazing. To be the leader of men. A prophet. She laughs kindly and says she doesn't think so. She likes to cook and clean and just be a good wife.

Then I realize what makes her pupils so unusual is that they are red. Blood red. Very strange but very exotic and beautiful at the same time. Apparently it's caused by a recessive gene which originates in Greece. What a coincidence with a Greek god as a spirit consort. I suggest to my friend that he maybe starts taking pictures with a digital camera instead of his SLR as he might be surprised by what he sees. He does. And he is. The garden is like a firework display in his pictures and a large grey orb which we both agree is Hades is almost omnipresent.

10th October 2010

10.10.10. I am approaching the Tor with my new friend. My heart is thumping in my chest and the weird words are starting to spill from my mouth as I run up the 500 or so steps to the Tor. It is pitch black and the wind is howling as usual. I race ahead of him and take up the familiar position in the Tor. I am kneeling, staff in one hand, feeling pretty bloody Biblical if I'm honest. I am shouting in what sounds like Aramaic.

I am praying for salvation for the human race.

The phrase comes in to my head, 'A perfect storm is coming. You must warn everyone.' I am not in my body anymore. Shit, this has never happened like this before. I think of that old guy who used to walk up and down Oxford

Street every day with a sign saying 'The End Is Nigh'. Well it was for him as he died but surely I am not going to end up like him and wandering around, wild eyed, claiming the end is in sight. I am looking down on the Tor. I can see my bald patch *through* my hat. X-Ray paranoia. My friend is making a video of me as I sing, cry and laugh in let's call it Aramaic for the sake of argument.

It's 10/10/10 today. Neat numbers seem to have an effect here. 09/09/09 was the night of the Big Flash last year. I now have no clue what I am doing. Something else has taken over. I think about Moses, Jesus, the Archangels. A massive wave approaching. Shaking. Floods. The moon crashing into the earth. Images are being planted in my head. Then I am back in my body. I am lying flat on my face on the stones.

I draw myself up and strike my stick on the hard surface of the stones. Boom! Out goes the blue wave. Out across Somerset, England, and around the planet. I used to do this before a long time ago you know. In a previous life. Things quieten down, then stop. It's over. My phone bleeps a message. It's from Kate, my very psychic friend. It reads: "Please warn me when you are going to do that. I just fell off the sofa." After our trip to Glastonbury my new friend never talks to me again so he isn't a new friend for very long. Shame.

18th November 2010

In Louisiana to make a documentary about the Deepwater Horizon accident and the aftermath of the impact locally. It's looking like quite good news for the Gulf Of Mexico generally from an ecological viewpoint. We take a trip through the bayous with a local prawn buyer and it smells sweet. The wind rustles the rushes and water fowl are in evidence.

It means I can visit New Orleans and see if the voodoo is as strong as they say. I don't have the sense when we are there that it is anymore. Maybe it's because Hurricane Katrina gave it such a kicking. Bourbon Street still rocks and reveals some vivid orbs floating around the bars where live blues pumps away all night long. I love the vibe in the French Quarter. A fun town with an upbeat mood. Apparently you can't go into the districts which are still in ruins after Katrina. Stray in there after dark and you won't come out. Maybe that's what I'm missing with the voodoo. I have a sort of death wish but not that bad. I feel comfortable with the history and atmosphere of the place. In fact I love it.

Archangel Uriel reminds me he is always watching over me in a blues bar off Bourbon Street, New Orleans. I think General Missy Blanch took this!

And just in case there's any doubt, he stays in the centre of the picture so I can photograph him again

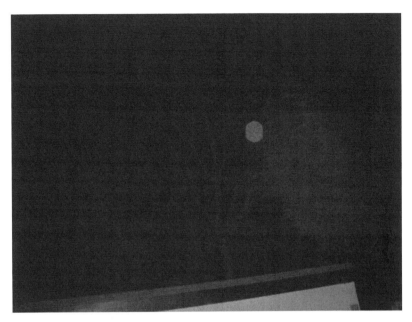

For reference with the New Orleans shot I took this in London on the night of the March Supermoon 2011. This is Uriel, the Archangel of Protection against Floods and Earthquakes. I had returned from the Japanese earthquake a few days earlier. He appeared in four consecutive photos that night.

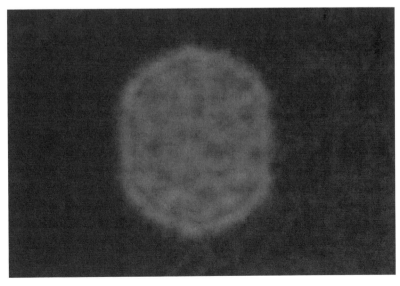

And the same image blown up. Exactly the same as the first appearance on my roof on pages 11 and 12.

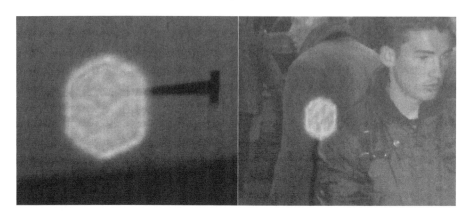

It's fascinating to see Archangel Uriel appearing in locations all over the world and a four year time span. I took these four pictures on my roof, in Kosovo, in a pub on Dartmoor and a hotel room in Glastonbury.

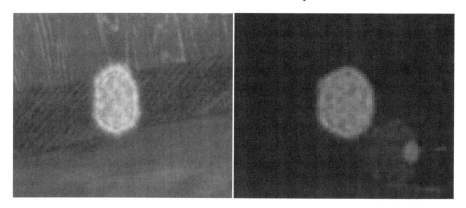

12th December 2010

A word about my friend Missy Blanch. I mentioned Missy way back at the start of my diary. This woman has been my guardian angel for years. This can also be described as my producer.

When I have been ill like I was all the way round Arizona, she cared for me.

She keeps my spirits up when I get a dose of the bi-polars. We are all blessed with angels and she is one of mine.

Always smiling, always happy. Blessings, General Missy and thank you.

She is with me in Louisiana. We are driving from Houston to New Orleans again and I feel wretched. Really, really bad and I have no idea why apart from the usual nagging sadness I sometimes suffer from.

Later I find out the Tree of Life in Glastonbury has been cut down with a chain saw. Someone is trying to damage the hold good and the Angels have on Glastonbury and make way for their own lords and masters who I sense might be the Ancient Egyptian gods like Set and Osiris.

The tree is said to have been planted by Jesus when he visited Glastonbury on a voyage around the known world with his uncle Joseph of Arimathea who was a merchant. The first Christian church was started in the centre of what is now Glastonbury. It was built so the Romans wouldn't find it from branches which formed a canopy by, it is said, Joseph and Jesus. The tree is said to have been planted at the same time. I have visited it many times in the past. It was decorated with thousands of coloured ribbons like a Mongolian or Tibetan shrine.

 And now so some idiot has crept up to it in the dead of night and chainsawed it down at its base. When I find out the news and know that it is this which has been tearing at me, I look in my mind to see who was responsible. And I see who it is. I call my friend Cherie who is an expert at distance viewing and tell her what I've seen. She says she saw the same person. Hardly what you can base a police report on though. He'll have to face what he's done at some point though.

People always do. The forces of Ancient Egypt are making their claim to the Tor as a result of the disruption. Disruption in the Middle East is coming because the Earth Chakras are opening and creating a desire for truth and fairness. And high food prices. This will only intensify. The ancient controls that the entities the Pharoahs in Egypt revered are looking for ways to keep their stranglehold intact on their people. They are seeking other springboards and the Tor is one as it is such a powerful portal.

The Louisiana A-team: me (before losing three stone) , cameraman Paul Lang, sound recordist Paul Miller and General Missy Blanch.

This was in the Crisis Centre at BP HQ in Houston where the Deepwater Horizon accident was worked on by hundreds of people. It would still be leaking if these four had been in charge.

14th December 2010

I have felt a strong desire to perform a ceremony for Louisiana and the longer I am there, the stronger the conviction becomes. One of my crew, an absolutely lovely guy, I sense was a brutal, murdering rapist in a past life. I tell him this over breakfast (never been that good at choosing my moment) about my feeling. His face drops and he looks at me silently for some time, weighing something up.

Then he tells me that he has a recurring dream where he tears off the arm of a girl and rapes her while she is dying. Suddenly the pancakes don't look so appetizing. I explain that this is a past life memory and that his contract in this life is to make amends and spread only love and laughter. Which is exactly what he does for the entire shoot and in his life at home. He does however have a nervousness about engaging with women he meets and it's my sense this is tied in with the monster he was in his previous life.

He is scared of engaging because of the memory he has of who he was. This sort of past life connection affects a lot of us and produces emotions and reactions we can't adequately explain as they skew our responses. Understanding who you *were* helps understand who you *are* so much. I have found a clearer picture of my own past lives has helped me define my own life and who I am. It explains so much about irrational, misplaced fears and emotions which don't sit well with your personality.

As a cleansing exercise, I invite my ex-murderer crew member to stand with me by the Mississippi outside New Orleans while I perform a ceremony. I can feel he is nervous as we walk away from the others who are busy filming a massive freighter steaming up the river. I click into Quetzalcoatal, my Maya spirit guide and perform the ceremony on the bank of the river. Apparently a small alligator makes a break for it just below us halfway through. I am a long way away amongst the stars presenting a petition to the Galactic Elders on behalf of the people of Louisiana to give them respite from hurricanes, oil spills and voodoo.

The petition is gravely accepted by the Elders and lodged. As we climb back in the enormous SUV we are using as a crew vehicle I am happy and content. Things will get better for Louisiana and New Orleans.

11th January 2011

I found myself alone in the Egyptian Room tonight at the British Museum in London. 11/01/11. Another one of those freakishly neat dates and another amazing experience. The energy from Ancient Egypt is getting more powerful. I don't trust it personally. Their gods Set, Anubis and Osiris are my enemies dating back to previous lives when I was an Israelite in Egypt. Set and Anubis are depicted as jackal-headed gods which are too close to draconian "preying mantis" imagery for my liking. Or the Nephilim – of course. That makes total sense. Perhaps all that Egyptian iconography is a rendition of the Nephilim too.

I had just been to a private viewing of the Egyptian Book of the Dead at the British Museum and on the way out looked in on the Egyptian Room where there is an impressive collection of Egyptian Curios. There were some powerful orbs around and every shot I took featured something. Incredible to have the place to myself.

This orb is very clear. It's hexagonal so it must be radiating and it's holding the energies contained in these stones in check. It could be Gabriel as it is quite distinct. (Location Courtesy British Museum)

Archangel Metatron is in this picture. My sense is that the energies are being held in check as opposed to being protected. (Location Courtesy British Museum)

15th March 2011

I am in Japan. There has been a really serious earthquake of 9.0 magnitude four days ago. That is big. I watched in horror on the news the previous Friday as the resulting tsunami washed across north-eastern Japan around Sendai. Lorries and cars on the roads were swept away like matchsticks. Ships weighing hundreds of tons were smashed into bridges and destroyed. The damage was unbelievable as a 10 metre high wave swept across the flat low lying farmland in the Sendai and Fukushima prefectures.

Tokyo is eerily quiet and empty. The inhabitants of this great city are staying at home. The train from the airport has stopped running so I take a cab on a journey which normally takes two hours or more. 45 minutes later I am at my hotel.

As I lie awake that night in the hotel I feel the presence of Michael and Uriel, the Protector and the Archangel of floods and earthquakes. They tell me I cannot stay in Japan for long and that we will not be able to complete my intended mission. There is too much danger from new earthquakes and radiation.

The Fukushima nuclear power plant has been inundated by the tsunami and damaged by the quake. It is currently on fire and the spent fuel rods are boiling dry. With the cooling pumps inoperable, there is a real chance the entire network of six reactors will explode and melt down.

I fall asleep but am woken by what I think are the couple in the room next door enjoying some noisy sex but the banging sound is my headboard, not theirs. The hotel is swaying and rocking as a series of pulses thump through it. These aftershocks continue over the next day.

Compared to Haiti, I am expecting this shoot for Channel Four back in the UK to be much easier logistically but we are told there is little fuel to get around by car, even helicopters are short of aviation fuel and they are not being allowed into the disaster area unless they are on a rescue mission so rescue teams can listen for the tiny sounds of any survivors calling for help. Food and water is running out in a large area outside the affected area as the roads are blocked and there is no where to stay. Haiti all over again.

16th March 2011

The danger from the reactors is worsening and people are being advised to leave the country if they can. Japan feels like a very dangerous place to be as the problems are far from over. Generally once a fault line has had a big release, it quiets down after a few aftershocks over the following days. But the subduction zone off Honshu, the main island of Japan, isn't.

There is an aftershock every 15 minutes or less and we are five days into the quake. This must mean the fault line is still moving. This is after Japan moved three metres to the east and then back a metre. The north eastern area has dropped a metre in height. The earth has shifted a metre on its axis and slowed its rotation a tiny yet measurable amount. That is a very big shift indeed.

Roger Bilham, my partner in seismological crime, has arrived from his home in Colorado. He is overexcited and very pleased to be here from a scientific point of view. We plan a flight up to Akita then a chopper ride into the disaster area to study the aftermath and look for geological clues about what the quake has done to the land.

We know that the cause is submerged a hundred miles off eastern Japan under the sea where one side of the two fists of the subduction zone between the tectonic plates has sprung up and dislodged the sea along the coastline.

The death toll is rising. In fact it takes a leap when half a town of 19,000 souls is reported as missing, presumed dead. I wonder if my job here, as well as documenting the science for Channel Four with Roger, is another soul rescue experience.

Michael and Uriel say not. The ancestors of the dead who the Japanese are very actively connected to have the situation wonderfully in hand. But they say I am there to protect Tokyo from a second big quake like the one which destroyed the city in 1923. There is a second fault line off Tokyo called the Tokia fault which is under enormous load and must be contained.

The lesson for me on this trip is to wield the power of the ark of the covenant for the first time. They say I will know the moment.

Roger and I take a helicopter flight from Tokyo and head out over this spectacular city toward the affected area.

As we are landing back in Tokyo at the heliport the pilot hears over the radio that we have probably just flown through the radioactive plume from Fukushima and that there is a live earthquake taking place. Roger is almost beside himself with excitement as we film him in the heli.

As we land there are cracks in the tarmac which are oozing sand. This is because the water in the ground beneath is being squeezed and stretched by the force of the quake and it is being turned into an earthy milkshake by the pressure in a process known as liquefaction.

In the van heading back to the hotel I know it is the moment to invoke the ark. I say a silent prayer to cloak Tokyo in Michael and Uriel's protective shield and ask for the power of the ark of the covenant to safeguard Tokyo from the destructive power of the scar in the earth 100 miles off the coast.

The Ark of the Covenant which is hidden through a gateway accessed from Glastonbury Tor. This is what I visualized in Tokyo to protect the great city. My sister thinks I'm nuts to talk about this sort of thing. But it hasn't been hit has it?

Roger Bilham at the start of our helicopter ride into a radioactive cloud in Japan.

I took this en route to the north from the helicopter of the smouldering remains of the LPG plant in Tokyo which was still burning 5 days after the earthquake.

The Message

The Maya people, who lived in Mexico and Guatemala for thousands of years then seemed to almost completely vanish in about 800 AD, are resonating in my head. No self-respecting New Ager can avoid a fascination with the ancient peoples of South America. The Incas, the Aztecs and the Maya demonstrated a grasp of astro-physics, astrology and mysticism which is admirable even today.

What is genuinely so fascinating about them was their use of the Long Count Calendar. This is the most accurate calendar ever devised without the aid of modern devices like the atomic clock in Greenwich, London, which is accurate to millionths of a second.

They, as far as we know, had no such instruments apart from a clever geared ancient slide rule. They were able to accurately predict the position of our solar system in relation to the rest of the Universe over a precise period of 5125 years. This also helped them plan for increases in solar activity which affects the weather and therefore farm crops and allowed them to plan for lean years.

Why they disappeared is a mystery but it is thought it was a combination of the impact of invading nations from elsewhere – the Spanish and the Danes were in South America centuries before Columbus landed and 'discovered' America again for Spain – and that they died from disease and famine. The Maya knew the sun switches its north and south pole every 11.5 years and goes through a cycle of increasing solar intensity of about the same period.

The solar maximum as it is called which occurs every 11 to 14 years has a considerable impact on the earth. The greatest modern threat is to communications and the power supply, which a big solar storm can disrupt.

Mass coronal ejections caused by the rotation of the sun which acts like an electrical dynamo leap away from the sun and flow out into space. They are released when the sun's electro magnetic field can no longer hold them. They contain almost unimaginably powerful blasts of energy which if released towards our planet 93 million miles away bathe us in cosmic rays, also known as the solar wind.

It's not a wind as we know it in our atmosphere. This is what causes the northern lights, the aurora borealis. We are protected thanks to the Van Allen belt and other electro magnetic shields which surround the earth. If they weren't there, we would fry in the radiation. I have discovered recently that there might be a correlation between increases in solar storms and the triggering of major earthquakes. There has been a significant solar storm a few days before every single major earthquake in recent years. These include Indonesia, Pakistan, China, Haiti, Chile, New Zealand and Japan.

Of course, there are solar storms regularly but the connection seems to be pretty direct. And when there is a major quake, something called dynamic triggering sometimes takes place. This means subsequent quakes quickly run round the tectonic plate system where the quake originated in a knock-on effect. The earth's crust is an arrangement of plates which slide and grind against each other over millions of years. They move at about the same speed as the rate your fingernails grow but the pressure they exert on one another causes sections to suddenly move from time to time and that gives the quake. They create mountain ranges like the Himalayas and the Rockies.

The Maya understood this and they had a three-dimensional mapping system of the heavens. When you consider the implication of that it is mind-blowing. How did they know that not all those lights in the sky were the same distance away? Astronomy is mind boggling. The nearest star to us, Alpha Centauri, is 4.5 billion light years away. Our own sun is a mere 8 minutes at the speed of light. That is a huge differential. The nearest galaxy to ours, Andromeda, is 2 million light years away.

The Maya knew we would return to exactly the same place we occupied in our solar system's rotation round the centre of the Milky Way on December 21st 2012 which we occupied exactly 26,000 years earlier. How the hell did they work this out? Because they are spot on.

This is also the day their 5125 year long calendar finishes and there isn't another one to follow. A lot of doom mongering has been written on this subject and it's not necessarily the only outcome. But there are factors which suggest there is some sort of cosmic U-turn approaching. And this fact is the message the angel realm are asking me to share with you so you are prepared. There, I've said it. That feels better now it's out. Phew.

I think the Maya were able to download their information in the way I, and others like me, can. It's not necessarily scientific. It's not based on calculation. It's not there one minute but it is the next. Ever since I found myself floating around above my own body on the Tor, it's been there. So having received the message, I have been looking for a more scientific context to help explain it you as best I can in the most logical way.

And this is what I have found out, partly from my work making science documentaries and partly from new research.

Large solar flares cause clouds to form and promote more rain which can lead to flooding. Solar flares possibly can trigger earthquakes. No scientist will yet confirm this link but I know it's correct based on my own observations of their occurrence.. Our own magnetic poles slowly flip every few million years. 40 times or so in the last 75 million years. The north pole is currently moving position toward Russia at about 40 miles per year. Not a huge rate but it is increasing.

We can tell when the poles have flipped, in case you are wondering how we can possibly know what the poles were doing millions of years ago, by studying sediments. Deposits in ice, soft muds in the oceans' lifeless abyssal plains which are huge, and in rock, tell us everything we need to know about the earth's history. And when the poles flip what are known as chaotic sediments are left. In other words all sorts of muck is suddenly laid down as the event causes chaos. Like floods and tidal waves which wash right round the earth.

For this to happen, the poles would need to flip in a matter of hours which scientists tell us is unlikely. But the sediments tell another story.

The Maya were also very aware of the position of the planets during the equinoxes and solstices. They believed that when the planets were in a straight line like a celestial cat's cradle, this also had an effect on disruption on earth. Scientists believe this theory is nonsense but I think they are quite brave to take this view bearing in mind how accurate the Maya were on most things.

I am told that a vast body like Jupiter has a millionth of the gravitational effect which the moon by comparison has on shifting the world's oceans up and down with the tides. We have lived with the tides all our lives. It feels normal and acceptable. But someone worked out that if you gave a scientist the data relating to the earth and the moon's mass, the 240,000 mile distance between them and their gravitational fields, the slide rule answer on the potential effect of the moon on the tides would be one or two centimetres difference between high and low tide. Not 3 metres. So that's a margin of error of 9000% or so.

I have been conducting my own research on the effect of planetary alignment, solar activity and earthquake frequency. When the sun, moon, earth and perhaps mercury or mars are in alignment, and there is also heightened solar flare activity, earthquake frequency and 5.0 magnitude plus quakes also shoot up. In the 12 hours around the Dec 21st Solstice in 2010 and the January 6 2011 lunar eclipse which included mercury in alignment, earthquake activity of 5.0 magnitude plus increased by a factor of 10.

I have received email notifications from USGS (US Geological Survey) of all quake activity for three years and have developed a good feel for the ebb and flow but this was astonishing to watch unfold. With a solar storm hitting the earth, as the eclipse approached at 7.40 am on January 6th 2011, the quake activity climbed then subsided slowly. And the question is why aren't scientists noticing the same anomalies? It's because they aren't looking. You would be amazed by how such intelligent, brilliant brains can only see as far as their own discipline. A truly wonderful example of paradigm blindness.

Now, there is no significant planetary alignment forecast for Dec 21st 2012 according to the predictor the University of Calgary in Northern Ireland use. But the UK Meteorological Office, NOAA and AAA in the US are predicting an early solar maximum instead of the original estimate of 2014 of around…December 2012. But there is however a total solar eclipse due on November 13th 2012. That means the sun, moon and the earth will be in alignment. The Maya knew something. Perhaps they elected to leave the planet altogether in 800 AD as they foresaw what would happen. Their Long Count calendar commenced just after the year Noah's flood is thought to have receded.

I am charged with telling you these things and you must decide what to do about them for yourself. I was at a lecture last night by a learned space weather expert speaking to an audience of some of the UK and the world's finest brains in physics. He knows about solar flares and the effect they can have on the planet. Business is being educated about the potential cost more and more.

The UK's Prime Minister David Cameron asked for a detailed space weather briefing recently he said. The speaker then ran through some headlines he had found about the solar maximum causing disruption and the potential effect on GPS, communications, power and computers. One headline in particular struck a chord with me. It was about there being a perfect storm in 2012.

In other words, a confluence of factors resulting in sudden intense flooding or a series of earthquakes, or a tidal wave which could reach right round the world. The Indonesian tsunami went right round the planet three times. Everyone at the presentation in the academic wood-panelled room chortled indulgently and the presentation moved on.

But the perfect storm has been a phrase which has been on the tip of my tongue for months. What if a solar storm happened to coincide with a freak planetary alignment, a sudden shift in our poles, a shift in the sun's magnetic poles and an island like the volcanic Cape Verde in the Atlantic collapsing into the ocean?

They have been waiting for that to happen to Cape Verde for 600 years and so far it has deposited 250 cubic kilometres of rock down the long smooth slope north of the island. If the whole island breaks up and collapses as predicted, due to an earthquake or its volcano waking up, it could create a tidal wave 400 metres high which would hit west Africa, the UK and the east coast of the US.

Or if the Katla volcano erupts in Iceland.

It would dwarf its sister which erupted recently and historically has erupted within three years. Katla could plunge the earth into a winter lasting years as its ash would block out the sun's rays. It's very big. It took us twenty minutes to skidoo across its bowl (the bit which erupts and would blast ice chunks the size of cars onto Reykjavík) at 40 kph.

I have the sense that there is going to be some sort of a freak storm on a global scale around that time. 13,000 years ago a solar flare flash baked the moon and the earth. Half the large mammals in North America disappeared at the same time, probably as a result of the solar storm.

This cycle of change is already well under way and it is not coincidence that the last decade nature without precedent has struck blow after blow on humanity. As well as the celestial significance, much of what is happening is rooted in science. But because we have distanced science and the soul, the two elements are in conflict instead of in harmony.

2012 is a key year in this – for solid scientific reasons.

The Maya knew this when they started the Long Count Calendar 5124 years ago. They had received celestial knowledge about astronomy, astrophysics and astrology I believe from an ancient race called the Nephilim. They knew the factors even then which would combine to produce a perfect storm in 2012 to test the human race.

This is not something governments wish you to know but you deserve to. It's why the Roman Catholic church incredibly is staging an inquisition in Peru right now. They are still trying to suppress the shaman descended from the Incas, Aztecs and Maya who know the truth.

It's not a very palatable truth, but consider the following.

The sun's magnetic poles will flip in 2012, causing a large increase in solar activity. This happens every 11.5 years and creates the solar maximum when solar flares can increase in intensity by a magnitude of 10.

Our protective shields which prevent us from being killed within 30 minutes from the effects of solar radiation have been damaged by the electro magnetic fields we produce in our power grids.

Solar radiation is thought to increase earthquake activity. It also encourages cloud formation. Water droplets form around positively charged matter arriving from the sun called hygroscopic particles which can increase the intensity of rain and cause floods.

I have discovered there has been a significant solar flare within a few days of every single major quake which has affected populated areas since the Indonesian quake in 2004.

The position of our moon and other planets is also thought to trigger quakes. There was a supermoon 10 days after the Indonesian earthquake when the moon was 13% closer to the earth than normal. This also happened 8 days after the Japan earthquake.

In the four hours around the December solar eclipse and January lunar eclipse this year where the sun, moon and earth were in line, there was a tenfold increase in earthquake activity of more than 4.0 magnitude on the Richter scale.

In December 2012 we will be at the solar maximum where there is the possibility that a solar flare will actually reach the earth, as it did about 14,000 years ago when the moon and the earth were "flashbaked". We will be at our closest point to the black hole at the centre of the Milky Way where its massive gravitational pull on the earth will be at the strongest it's been for 26,000 years.

The Maya calendar ends next year. In the Lost Book of Nostradamus, he drew his last ever picture. It's one of him holding a blank page with 2012 End Of Days written on it.

This period of disruption in nature has already begun. We are in it now. It won't be the end of us, but it is going to be a rough ride and we need to be prepared and call on the angels for their help. That is the message the angels want us to hear and that is how I end the diary.

Now it's up to us to will it not to happen. This is possible. Anything is possible. Music can change the molecular composition of water. For it to happen we must conquer our fear, the darkness, the evil which is waiting to consume us. We need to change fundamentally in the way we live and think. We need to wake up.

I think the Maya knew another huge solar storm might hit on December 21st 2012. Look what happens every time there is a big coronal mass ejection or solar flare – it is followed by a big earthquake a few days later. True of New Zealand and Japan and, according to my own research, every other major earthquake which has affected the human race in the 21st century. Scientists are still saying earthquakes are only affected by the centre of the earth but they're looking in the wrong place. The sun is connected to earthquakes.

Scientists do not know everything and they are not always right.

Find me another decade which has had so many direct hits on us by nature. This is not the sort of thing anyone wants to hear. No one thanks you for telling them. But why do you think there are so many orb pictures turning up anyway? Why people like me are being overwhelmed by the presence of angels, and who are disturbed by their agitation? I didn't ask for this to happen to me and, in a way, I wish it hadn't as it has turned my world upside down. Your governments don't want to cause panic as a result of becoming aware of this because control will be lost.

But how is that the remains of 15 metre high giants can be unearthed, a UFO can hover over King David's Mount in Jerusalem and be filmed by half a dozen different people, Nostradamus's Lost Book can contain a final blank page depicting 2012 and these events not be front page news, when death and murder are daily?

Who or what do you think is controlling the media and our leaders? You must decide these things for yourselves, draw your own conclusions and act. Just remember always, the angels are with you. Call on them for help and they will come.

If the human race turns to the light like a field of sunflowers turning toward the sun's warm rays and renounces the dark, the fear, the negative, who knows what we can achieve or change? Nothing is set in stone and we can triumph by choosing love over hatred, peace over conflict. There is a simple logic to survival. If you outlive your usefulness, you perish. We see it in nature and history. We must evolve as a race and very quickly.

Most of us are amazing beings and deserve better than the world we have created for ourselves.

Lady Gaia will shrug us off like she has many times before unless we change.

Blessings and may God's love be with you.